Praise for Boxtree's Motley Fool books, from experts and ordinary readers:

The Motley Fool UK Investment Guide, amazon.co.uk's number one bestseller:

'(The book) is geared entirely to the UK market and it is difficult to see how anyone could fail to benefit.' *Mail on Sunday*

'This book has completely changed the way I look at the world of personal finance … I can't recommend this book enough: funny and informative.' P. Coleman

The Motley Fool UK Investment Workbook

'The most useful investment book of 1999.' *Mail on Sunday*

'If you've ever wondered if you needed a pension, whether shares are as risky as they sound or if you simply can't figure out where all your pay cheque went this month, this is an ideal introduction to making your money work for you.' Tim Jordan

The Fool's Guide to Investment Clubs

'A good, easy to understand introduction to investment clubs.' Darron Welch

The Motley Fool UK Web site is the winner of the 1999 *New Media Age* Award for Best Personal Finance Web site and the 1999 *Creative Freedom* Best Electronic Media Site.

The following Motley Fool books are also published by Boxtree:

The Motley Fool UK Investment Guide
The Motley Fool UK Investment Workbook
The Fool's Guide to Investment Clubs
The Fool's Guide to Online Investing
Make Your Child a Millionaire: The Fool's Guide
(available soon)

How to Invest When You Don't Have Any Money: The Fool's Guide

Christopher Spink

BOXTREE

First published 2000 by Boxtree
an imprint of Macmillan Publishers Ltd
25 Eccleston Place, London SW1W 9NF
Basingstoke and Oxford

www.macmillan.co.uk

Associated companies throughout the world

ISBN 0 7522 7168 7

9 8 7 6 5 4 3 2 1
A CIP catalogue record for this book is available from
the British Library.

Typeset by Jane Coney
Printed in Great Britain by Mackays of Chatham plc, Kent

p.103 Extract from 'The Less Deceived' by Philip Larkin used by kind permission of
The Marvell Press, East St. Kilda, Australia

Contents

Preface   7

Foreword: Foolish Alchemy   11

How to read this book: Foolish directions   13

Introduction: Welcome to the Fool!   17

Chapter 1 Debt around your neck   23

Chapter 2 Cash in hand   45

Chapter 3 Pay in your pocket   66

Chapter 4 A roof over your head?   80

Interlude: Who wants to be a millionaire?
(I don't! I don't!)   97

Chapter 5 The pension problem   103

Chapter 6 The Foolish alternative to pensions   124

Chapter 7 Be maniacally mechanical and
meticulously methodical!   141

Chapter 8 The jewel in the Foolish investment
crown: buying a part of individual
companies   156

Conclusion: Then you'll be a Fool my son …   189

Acknowledgements   192

Contents

Preface

Everyone invests. Most of us just don't realize it. But think about the huge amount of time, effort and perhaps money we all spend on developing our friendships, jobs and lifestyle. You could definitely call these pursuits canny investing, since hopefully they have given us a great return. So you would think that with all this investing experience we should be experts at money management! Er … Dream on … But it is possible to make investing easy, painless and fun.

When it comes to funding our activities, a lot of us would prefer to turn off and leave the financial planning and juggling act to someone else, letting them invest on our behalf. And yet have you noticed that, despite this leap of faith, there never seems to be enough cash to do everything you want? So let's turn this assumption on its head and imagine handing over responsibility for all your day-to-day affairs to someone else. You wouldn't want your bank manager organizing your social life, now would you?

Whatever you want to accomplish in life, whether it is going on holiday, buying a house, raising children, even retiring, money rears its ugly head somewhere in the planning. And as we all know, bank notes don't grow on trees. However, don't worry too much because, if planted properly, even the tiniest of savings can bud into a magnificent cash crop, sufficient to meet most needs. And it needn't take much time to bed down this plan. You, too, can simply plot your way to financial security.

The Motley Fool does not broadcast this message alone. It blares out from every direction: the Government urges you to save, financial firms implore you to save, your parents say you must save. Meeting and accepting the problem is the easy bit; it is still far from easy to solve. Making a start is tremendously hard, especially if debts also demand your immediate attention. Even if you are in this precarious position, however, you will still be harassed from all angles to start this pension, pay off that debt, open this account, use that card. Confronted by this wise advice, what should you do and how should you go about it?

Perhaps the first thing we should answer is not what you should invest in, and how, but *why* you should invest at all.

Most obviously, if you don't you won't be able to do all those things you always dreamt of: going on holiday, buying a house, raising children or retiring. Well you could, but your exact choice in these matters might become severely limited. For instance you could probably just about make it down to Margate and back for the weekend. You might scrape together enough for what estate agents describe as a 'surprisingly spacious studio in an up-and-coming neighbourhood', but is in fact a cramped and poky bedsit above the local kebab joint. And, courtesy of the state, you might get by on £66.75 per week when you give up work. Oh … and that's before the extra demands that children (the little angels) bring.

The prospect doesn't sound exactly enticing, does it? So what else is on offer? Well, a surprising amount actually. But considering it's all designed to achieve the simple task of increasing your wealth, most of it appears astonishingly confusing for the novice. Let's look at the problem – you want to save money whilst you are earning so that when you are on holiday, at home or retired, you can still live as you wish. Why does that seem so hard to achieve? Well, as no doubt you are aware, there are many people who make a living from 'solving' these sorts of financial problems – who also charge a price for their privileged information. Here at the Fool we call such parasites 'the Wise' for their blinding use of jargon to sell you completely underwhelming, unsatisfactory, overly expensive but poorly performing investment products: all far from Foolish.

For instance a Wise adviser might suggest that you borrow to achieve some of these aims. He (or of course the little devil could be a she) might suggest that you put the holiday on the credit card, take out a 100 per cent mortgage, or go to the bank with begging bowl in hand when the first tot appears. But this clever strategy would prove punitively expensive and cripple you in the process. As for a happy retirement, forget it.

Ah, yes, those blissful carefree years when you can forget the nine-to-five grind and concentrate on the more pleasant joys of life. This independent idyll is what we hanker after and is the main aim of most investors. You could take out a pension, I suppose. But before you do so, just remember that the main aim of most Wise salesmen offering such products is to receive a percentage of the funds you wish to invest. Canny business huh? Selling you dreams on the back of your insecurity.

Before signing away your savings to one of the dozens of providers all too willing to welcome you and your cash into their lair, first consider the different options open to you. This is important, after all – it's your future. The paths are various and twisted. It might seem a hopelessly long trek, but don't despair. You can overcome these obstacles simply, with only a little effort and time.

By saving small amounts regularly in a variety of simple schemes, you can easily turn £100 a month into a £1,000,000 pot within thirty-nine years. Yes, unbelievably, by setting aside a little each month and never withdrawing from your investment pile, your savings can grow effortlessly into substantial amounts. This is the miracle of compounding your returns. To become a millionaire, all you need to do is find an investment scheme that pays a net return of 12 per cent annually, and put £100 a month into it for thirty-nine years! (This calculation assumes a constant inflation rate of 3 per cent and that you have sheltered the investments in tax-free schemes. If you pay basic income tax on your earnings, you'd have to put £220 a month into the scheme to get to £1,000,000).

Jump for joy! If you can't wait much longer and want to discover more about this mind-blowing miracle and mouthwatering prospect, skip to page 39 for a sneak preview, including an explanation and more details of such schemes.

In the meantime, think of your savings arena as an allotment patch, overgrown by a jungle of jargon. If you have debts, consider your patch to be also covered in weeds of various descriptions. Your first aim must be to clear away the weeds, particularly the most choking ones, such as credit cards. Then, as the weeding process continues, you can start to slash back the jargon jungle and understand what you want to achieve.

Go down to the garden centre, or alternatively get online and shop electronically. Sift through the various products and pick the ones that will help you to achieve your goal. Be very careful of those purporting to help your patch grow more quickly, especially if proffered by a Wise salesman. These might be expensive fast-growing fertilizers, which boost your returns over the short term, but might in the long run poison and destroy your patch.

By keeping things simple, you will be in control of your own savings patch and be able to nurture your own future without falling victim to the Wise, who will gobble up unwary investors with their enticing array of glittering products. And, as most gardeners will tell you, the end results can prove most satisfying and rewarding. There is nothing like sitting back surrounded by the fruits of your labours, especially knowing that the effort has been yours and yours alone over many years.

Just as no one at the Fool will tell you how to live your life, at the end of the day it's up to you to decide how to organize your finances. This book won't tell you what to do. It's not a manual to follow rigidly. Instead it will offer suggestions which you can choose to follow if you wish. Take tips for free from anyone you meet, but remember that you're the one in control.

But first, before donning your gardening gloves and surveying your untended plot, a short Foolish foreword.

Foreword: Foolish Alchemy

Isaac Newton: the bloke in the wig under the apple tree, gravity, father of modern physics, blah, blah, blah. For most people the story ends there. In reality, however, Isaac was more of a sly old cove than these facts suggest. Far from being selflessly devoted to the laws governing objects in motion, he spent the vast majority of his life on another mission entirely: the transmutation of base metals into gold, known to you and me as alchemy. As we all know, he didn't succeed. So, you might ask, if someone as brainy as him couldn't pull off this stunt, how are you supposed to do something as seemingly impossible as invest with no money?

Pah! Ludicrous.

But hang on. Investing with no money is not alchemy. Rather, it's a state of mind. You may have no money now, or think you have no money, but if you don't start to think like someone focused on investing for your future, you'll probably never be in a position to do so. And that wouldn't do at all, because you would be squandering the chance to enrich yourself and provide securely for your future, while at the same time engaging in a uniquely interesting and compelling pastime.

In this book, Christopher Spink, one of the Motley Fool's most whimsical writers, leads you gently through the commonly accepted stages of investing without any money:

1. **Invest?! Stroll on, mate. I'm worse than skint. I'm up to my eyeballs in debt!**
2. **I just about keep my head above water, but money still seems to flow through my hands and there's nothing left at**

the end of the month. Oh, it's hopeless, hopeless, hopeless. In fact, I'm just so hopeless.

3. Actually, you know, I *could* put away £25 a month and still do all the things I like to do.

4. Hmm, looks like I'm starting to get a bit of a stash together, so now what?

5. This investing lark's quite fun. And a bit addictive too.

No one can pretend that this book will miraculously transport you from stages one to five with no effort on your part. What it can do, though, is show you a path. It can show you that it is possible, whatever stage you may be at, for you to get to the point where you become an investor.

That's probably the most important thing to take away from this book: that you can do it and that things may not be as hopeless as they look. As a writer and guide for this task, which seems so insurmountable for many people, I can't think of anyone better than Chris. The chap's a Fool, through and through, a delight to work with and be around, whose writing flows with an ease that frankly makes me green with envy.

Oh. Did I say 'the most important thing'? Sorry, that's wrong. The most important thing you'll take away from this book is that gutta-percha golf balls cost less and fly further than featherie ones. But you'll have to read on to find out why.

David Berger
Co-Founder
Motley Fool UK
January 2000

How to read this book: Foolish directions

This short section will give you a brief guide to the book and tell you how to extract the information you want most efficiently. If you're already slightly confused about the repeated use of the word Fool and wondering what the hell this Foolish lark is all about, where it stems from and who exactly the Wise are, then please take a quick look at the introduction which explains this whole concept succinctly.

After the introduction, the curtain goes up and the book proper begins. The text is divided into two parts. The first half is designed primarily for someone who has no investments but only financial worries. If you have no cash and find that what spare money you have merely goes on staving off the demands of your creditors, then this part of the book is probably most relevant to you. It should help you to manage your financial affairs simply and without hassle, so that you are in control of your cash rather than feeling your cash is controlling you. Your financial worries will be solved! It will then offer you hints as to how to reach the point where you are ready to invest.

If you have no debts, have your money house in order but are wondering what to do with the scraps left over each month, then the second part of the book, starting at Chapter Five, is probably more useful for you. Here we survey the investment scene, assessing what is available and which products might prove most useful.

So let's look at the first half in more detail. The first chapter talks about debts, how to pay them off and in what order to tackle them. It also talks about which ones to avoid if you possibly can, and why debts in general can be detrimental to your savings and investment plans. We also introduce the magnificent concept of compound interest. This is miserable if you are in debt, but miraculous when you are in credit. Compounding makes your returns more munificent if you have money but, on the down side, makes any debts you have become more dastardly.

This debt discussion is followed by a chapter on cash gleaning. Here we look at various ways of painlessly (and Foolishly) economizing on vital and necessary services, like accommodation, household bills, food, clothing and the telephone. Having sorted out these major outgoings, you should have some free cash to luxuriate in as you wish. You might even consider – wait for it – investing some of this surplus, if you have paid off your debts.

If you are still strapped for cash, the third chapter looks at ways of boosting your income. We take a brief look at the modern workplace and how you can negotiate a better pay package. Alternatively, there are suggestions for making your hobby a money-spinner.

The final chapter in this first half delves into the murky world of property dealings. How many people have urged you to get on the property ladder? Before clambering on the first rung, consider the carefree benefits of renting over the hassles of buying. Buying a property is a big step, commonly involving more debt in the form of a mortgage. If done rashly (and Wisely) the 'bloody mortgage' can do more to stymie your investment plans than anything else. Have a look here before you take the plunge.

Before moving on to Foolish investment options, we take a short restful interlude. To put you at ease, we bring forth two people with masses of money who nevertheless managed to lose it all. Starting as a millionaire may not be as good an option as it's made out to be. Prince or pauper – the Fool knows which side of the financial fence he is on!

The second half of the book begins with two chapters about the pension problem. The first explains why the idyll of blissful and happy retirement might be harder to achieve using this vehicle than via other, more Foolish, options; the second explores these fantastic alternatives.

In Chapter Seven we move on to discuss cheap, simple and easy-to-follow mechanical methods of investment which have outperformed most professional money managers in the long run.

Finally, we take a look at the jewels in the Foolish investment crown. Inside this Aladdin's cave we discover why holding on to shares in some of the country's leading companies for reasonably long periods of time makes sense, and can lead you to financial security. We pinpoint the things to look for when choosing such glorious investments, give simple procedures to follow, and explain why investing isn't gambling. The mysteries of investment clubs and finding a broker to execute your decisions cheaply are also unveiled, as is an inexpensive method of backing the best companies without using a broker at all.

Above all, Foolishness encourages a questioning attitude. This is to prevent you from becoming ensnared in the conventional lines spun by Wise professional financial salesmen. In this spirit, the chapters are discursive essays that try to explain the worst problems clearly, suggest how to avoid them and outline what better solutions are around instead.

All chapters or sections can be looked at in isolation, as they cover self-contained topics. Throughout the text you will find practical advice sections, which elaborate specific points; in the first few chapters, there are some sections designed specifically for students. And don't forget that at the end of each chapter you will also find a summary of the main points discussed.

If after reading the book you want to read about more Foolish investment ideas, then the Motley Fool has written several other relevant volumes, details of which can be found at **www.fool.co.uk**. Have fun Fooling around!

Introduction: Welcome to the Fool!

The Queen was in a furious passion, and went stamping about,
shouting, 'Off with his head!' or 'Off with her head!' about once
in a minute.
Lewis Carroll, *Alice in Wonderland*

So how do you invest when you don't have any money? You might well say, 'Impossible – you're having me on, aren't you?' If you were then told that a Fool was going to show you how to carry out this heroic task, no doubt you'd be even more sceptical. And with good reason. No one should tell you what to do with your hard-earned cash, because the person best placed to decide that can only be seen by you in a mirror. Go and take a look. Who is it? It's YOU.

Think about most other important decisions you make about your adult life – where to live; what job to do; who to live with; where to go on holiday; what to have for supper and which video to watch, amongst countless others. They all are, at the end of the day, your own choices, or at least they probably should be. So why, when it comes to money management, do so many people turn off and rely on others to do the thinking for them?

More worrying is that many of us actually pay these manager types expensive fees to lock up our cash away from us and out of our control. Crazy or what? This process may not necessarily make us rich, but regardless of whether the managed fund performs well or not, the collective fees fleeced from us and others like us certainly line the deep pockets of such 'professionals'.

Surprising numbers of us go weak between the ears when in the almighty presence of Wise financial advisers. However, with the advent of the Internet it is now possible to access as much financial information at home as they do in their palatial offices. Until relatively recently this wasn't the case. But now, when confronted by an adviser full of jargon, you can scythe through his bluffing with blinding statistics from the World Wide Web. More pointers to finding this knockout stuff will appear later in the book. Subtle hint: you could try the Motley Fool (**www.fool.co.uk**) for starters!

Don't be daunted by this prospect of do-it-yourself finances. By questioning the title of this book you are already getting into the Foolish frame of mind. Scoff away. This is your first step towards Foolishness. Questioning any financial advice you are offered is supremely Foolish. Fools are optimistic and honest individuals, with inquiring minds liberally dosed with common sense. They will not settle with anything less than the best for their own particular position and, importantly, they have fun finding out what that 'best' is with fellow Fools.

But briefly, by way of an explanation of this Foolish malarkey, a short scenic detour ...

A Foolish history lesson

Cast your mind back for one dreadful moment to some of the god-awful regimes that existed in the last century. Appalling places like Nazi Germany or Stalinist Russia spring to mind. In totalitarian states such as these, you couldn't stray from the party line and express your own views about anything much at all (apart from undying admiration for your leader, of course).

In the same way, no one was allowed to criticize the king in the medieval courts of Europe. Well, almost no one. Some lucky people could. You may remember that court jesters cropped up from time to time to sit beside monarchs. Jesters were also called fools. Shakespeare's plays have a whole flock of them. Fools, alone, were allowed to tell the king uncomfortable truths without having their heads lopped off for their impudence. Through their sharp comments, fools often made the king's brown-nosed and supposedly 'wise' advisers look extraordinarily dim-witted.

Thus fools played a vital part in court affairs and, despite their motley image, weren't just there for light relief. (No wonder, then, that King Lear is utterly distraught in the last scene of his eponymous play, when he finds that his 'poor fool' has been hanged by the usurpers who used to advise him Wisely at court.)

Consider how differently and more pleasantly the twentieth century might have turned out if fools had still been around to trip up the jack-booted dictators of the 1930s. So before dismissing this particular Fool from your court, transpose this scenario to modern times.

In 1993 two American brothers decided to revive the concept of the Fool. In a small town outside Washington DC, Tom and David Gardner set up a financial newsletter called the *Motley Fool*. The Gardners figured that all the fund managers and attendant advisers surrounding Wall Street were now the Wise advisers intimidating poor individuals, or fools (small f).

But by simply asking Foolish questions, the *Motley Fool* attempted to strip away the myth that only expensive Wise men could capably manage the monetary affairs of individual Fools (large F). Because in fact, many of the Wise were quite blatantly underperforming the market average return and charging large fees for this poor performance. From now on anyone deciding to look after their own money, via simple and understandable methods, was deemed to be making a Foolish (large F) move. The Wise advisers considered this foolish (small f).

Then something magical happened. The founding Fools found a new medium to transmit this Foolish financial message to the world: the Internet, also known as the World Wide Web. Thus the Motley Fool was born online at **www.fool.com**. Why was this special? Well, it enabled Fools to contact each other by swapping ideas and thoughts about long-term Foolish investment strategies and ways to avoid the wily traps of the Wise. Today more than a million people have registered with the US Motley Fool, swapping many thousands of messages daily.

In a wider context, the information available on the World Wide Web enabled a more effective campaign to be conducted against the privileged financial world of the Wise. Information on companies and investments, previously held in databases in stockbrokers' offices, could now be communicated directly from the companies themselves to individual investors. Also, the Web made it possible to reduce the transaction fees in many different deals, from buying books at Amazon.com to buying shares via discount brokers such as Charles Schwab – a process that is accelerating to this very day.

Meanwhile, across the Atlantic, furtive Foolish movements were occurring in William Shakespeare country, Folly's original homeland – Britain. Specifically, a GP from North Devon, Dr David Berger (who wrote the Foreword) was infiltrating the Motley Fool in the US. This came to the attention of the Foolish authorities (if indeed there are any) and a summit meeting followed between the two parties.

The founding Fools decided that the Foolish movement should be replicated in the UK, along with its three main aims – greater Foolish interaction between Internet users, via e-mail and messages; wider dissemination of financial and other information; and lower transactional costs online compared with traditional avenues. And so yes, the Motley Fool UK (**www.fool.co.uk**) started operating in October 1997 thanks to the hard efforts of Dr Berger and his trusty lieutenant Bruce Jackson.

Over two years later, four UK best-selling books have been published, and, by the end of 1999, over 100,000 British people had registered on the UK Web site, which offers continuous Foolish comment, information and data on investments and all other financial products. These Fools now swap on average well over a thousand messages each day on every topic under the financial sun. So if after reading this book you are intrigued by Folly, you can satisfy your hunger by getting online.

Apart from visiting the Motley Fool there are, of course, a million other things you can do on the Web. My particular favourites include playing live chess with insomniacs in New Zealand, conversing, via e-mail, with my cousin in Chile, browsing the *Encyclopaedia Britannica* for free, listening to Californian radio stations and following England's cricket fortunes via live commentary whilst at work. The world's your oyster online, so just get connected! But now, having explained the difference between the Wise and the Foolish, it's back to business.

Sore head?

What's your biggest headache on a day-to-day basis? Forget those little nags about never being able to find a seat on the train in the morning or your mother occupying your answerphone with inordinately long messages. The pain probably becomes more sharply defined towards the end of the month, when the bank balance starts to look decidedly thin. Does this lack of cash gnaw at you before payday? Does there never seem to be enough?

The throbs have no doubt become particularly harsh when a wise know-it-all pops up on the television screen to assault you with more worries about an old age of penury and poverty. Advisers everywhere are warning you to get a savings plan sorted or else. You know the scary stories – that Government funds alone won't tide you over in retirement. You want to laugh but inside you feel like crying at the impossibility of it all. If you have debts on top of all this, then your headache must be more like an incessant migraine.

You may not lose your head for political deviance nowadays, but if you don't organize your own financial scene, someone else will be willing to take control for a price. This is the heart of the problem. These thoughts are designed to make things seem worse than they are, so that you rush into making a hasty decision and fall helpless into the arms of the Wise.

But don't fret, because you're *Foolish*. You question things you're not sure about, and won't let people pull the wool over your eyes. And you know that time is on your side. If you have more debts than dosh then listen up. Sit down, take a deep breath, remember this isn't rocket science, and let's look at this thing Foolishly and logically.

First things first though, let's find some medicine for that headache …

Student grant?

To many people the quintessential student revolution happened in 1968, when protesters took to the streets of Paris to campaign against the Vietnam War, amongst other things. In fact, a deeper change has taken place over the past twenty years. Student numbers in the UK have increased almost tenfold. In 1979 only five per cent of 18-year-olds went on to any form of higher education. Now one in three do so.

The education of this vast student population costs towering amounts of money. So student tuition fees have been introduced and the student maintenance grant is gradually being phased out. Instead students are now invited to take out student loans from the Government, at preferential rates.

In short, the scenario is becoming more and more as it is in the US. Students have to pay their own way and are left with colossal debts at the end of their education. How, then, do you start your working life on a Foolish financial footing, when you are saddled with massive borrowings?

Whilst this book is hopefully relevant to all age groups, whatever their financial position, many Fools have suggested that students and graduates would find a study of investing without having any money particularly enlightening, since many are in this predicament. If you are still studying, you will hopefully find the Foolish principles useful as preparation for when you are in a position to pay off debts and start to invest for the future. Whilst at university, it might be best to concentrate on getting a degree and enjoying yourself as best you can when you're young.

However, the first half of the book is relevant to anyone who would like to have more cash than they do at present. The second half may be more useful for graduates, who are earning, than students, who are just barely making ends meet at university. Nevertheless there's no harm in getting ahead of the game and starting early. There are specific sections at the end of many chapters which students or recent graduates might find useful. Happy Fooling!

Chapter One – Debt around your neck

A recent survey asked what people most wanted to leave behind at the millennium. With a new age dawning, you may well have expected many noble replies. Horrors such as poverty, hunger, disease, child labour or famine might have topped the list. But no, most people surveyed thought quite naturally about their own predicaments. And a top-heavy 69 per cent said their personal debts were what they wanted to leave rotting back in the twentieth century.

This may seem callous, but it's not really dissimilar to the crusade by certain rock stars, celebrities and churches to get the Western world to forgive developing countries' debts in the year 2000. By becoming debt free, both individuals and nations have more liberty to decide what to do with their income: whether to spend, invest or donate it.

In this chapter we shall look at debts of any description. If you don't have any, congratulations, you can skip to Chapter Two. There we shall try to look at something altogether more appealing: how you spend your incoming cash each month and how you can make it Foolishly go further. Abracadabra!

By getting your own house in order, you can organize your life much more easily and decide exactly what to do with your surplus cash. If you don't do this, you end up merely handing it over to the bank to cover overdraft charges and interest payments. Unfortunately, most of us with debts can expect little forgiveness from such financial providers. We have to pay back the money we owe, with interest.

So before you can begin to invest you have to understand your current cash, or, more likely, *negative* cash position. This is because heavy debts could cripple your long-term investment plans. If you are paying exorbitant rates of interest then you will find it very hard to make any real return from the money you invest. Also, by looking at your own fascinating situation, you learn a lot about the basics of investing before you even begin. For example, by looking at the money the banks are making from your debt, you can understand what returns they are enjoying and how efficiently they are silting your hard-earned cash away from you. So take a deep breath. We're going to plunge in to try to work out this horrendous problem. You might find the experience enlightening. You should also find it educational.

If you are heavily in debt, you start at a considerable disadvantage, some way behind the starting line. In fact investments you make when in debt will have to outperform usual benchmarks by some distance if they are able to give you any real net increase in your worth. If you have £1,000 of debts increasing at, say, 10 per cent a month and savings of £1,000 rising at only 5 per cent a month, overall your debts will continue to rise at 5 per cent in the first month and more after that.

Investing whilst being indebted is like asking a top class sprinter to run the hundred metres with lead weights in his shoes. He would have to be able to run the distance shoeless in a world record time in order to make any impact when he has lead boots on. So it is with investments. If you start when you are laden with weighty debts, then you will waste all your effort trying to shake them off. So throw off the weights first, or at least get them under control.

And remember that your investment life should be more like a twenty-six-mile marathon than a hundred-metre sprint. Many people with heavy debts, apart from mortgages (of which more in Chapter Four) are reasonably young with plenty of time on their side. So if you're in this enviable position, relax a while, stretch and loosen up. You have a little leeway to rectify things.

You don't want to snap a hamstring in a mad opening dash and pull up short, out of the race, relying on the emergency services to pick you up. Instead, sort out your debts in the first mile, or even more Foolishly, stand still for the first ten minutes, planning your investment start, before flexing your financial muscles. This methodical strategy is far better than running in a silly, warm and hopelessly impractical fancy dress costume at a tremendous pace from the outset, only to collapse before getting even half-way round the course! You will see the more measured runner, who planned the twenty-six-mile race for ten minutes at the start, gliding smoothly past you at the first drinks stop.

This metaphor could run and run, but back to the nitty-gritty: how exactly do you begin? This is easier said than done. I think an example is needed.

Legal Luke's deft debt management

Take Luke, a lawyer. He left university five years ago with numerous debts. He owes £5,000 to the student loan company. This is a Government-backed debt, meaning that Luke has effectively borrowed £5,000 from the Government. The interest charged on this loan is, as you'd expect, very low and is generally the same as the current rate of inflation. The loan doesn't have to be paid back until his earnings reach £20,000 a year.

After university Luke went to law school for two years. His parents lent him £2,000 interest free, with no special repayment terms. But Luke also had to borrow money from his bank to fund the course. The bank was less generous than the Government or his parents.

He arranged a £6,000 graduate loan with the bank, which has a 10 per cent annual interest rate. This was repayable as soon as he finished the two-year course and started work. Having worked for three years, at a salary below £20,000, he now has £1,000 outstanding from this arrangement.

In addition to these loans, Luke has a £1,000 overdraft, which has a 15 per cent annual interest rate, and £1,000 of credit card borrowings, on which he pays interest of 20 per cent annually.

What should he do to get in a position to invest? Or, to put it more Foolishly, how should Luke manage his debts effectively?

Luke is like many professional people in their twenties. He tots up the total amount he owes and it comes to a frightening £10,000. This is made up of £5,000 in student loans; £2,000 from his parents; £1,000 graduate loan; £1,000 overdraft; and £1,000 credit card borrowings. At the same time he feels the need to start saving. Most lawyers have to fund their own pension and this issue is pressing hard on Luke. He would like to make a start on this long trek to retirement. What should he do? Which loans should he try to repay first?

The first thing to remember is that all these debts are different. They charge different rates of interest and each is repayable on a different time scale. Look at the interest rates first of all. The £5,000 student loan is effectively interest free, rising at only the rate of inflation – say 2 per cent per year. But this also means, perversely, that his debt to his parents, since they charge no interest at all, is already *falling* in real terms. Because of the effects of inflation, £2,000 today has less spending power than the £2,000 Luke was lent three years ago. In effect, Luke has saved £122 in interest payments to his parents, assuming that the inflation rate remains constant at 2 per cent each year.

Baffled? Let me explain.

If Luke's parents had charged interest at the rate of inflation in the first year, this would have added 2 per cent of £2,000, or £40, to the debt. This leaves Luke with £2,040 to pay after the first year. In the second year the addition would be 2 per cent of this £2040, or £40.80, leaving Luke with a total debt of £2,080.80, and in the third year 2 per cent of £2,080.80, or £41.62, would be added. Luke would now have to pay £2,122.42 all told. Thus the total interest payments at the rate of inflation on £2,000 over three years amount to roughly £122, or £40 + £40.80 + £41.62. But Luke's parents have waived this, because their loan is completely interest free. The £2,000 he will eventually have to pay back will be able to purchase far less than the £2,000 he was lent three years ago.

The graduate loan with the bank has to be paid back with interest of 10 per cent each year; the overdraft commands a rate of 15 per cent and the credit card borrowings charge an extortionate 20 per cent. These three interest rates far outstrip the 2 per cent and 0 per cent rates of the student and parental loans respectively.

Also, the student and parental loans differ from the other three borrowings because they are not arranged with strictly financial institutions. This is an important distinction. Luke's parents don't seem likely to send the bailiffs around to collect their £2,000 imminently. (In any case they wouldn't be able to, unless they could prove to the county courts that the terms of the borrowing agreement had been breached!) And that wouldn't be a very parental thing to do. Similarly, Luke doesn't have to pay off his student loan to the Government agency until his salary rises above £20,000. This should allow him to sit back and forget about these debts for the moment. He should lodge them at the back of his mind.

The graduate loan, overdraft and credit card borrowings are all repayable to a financial institution or bank of some description. These fish can prove much trickier to grapple with. The first thing is to know your enemy. Luke is dealing with two financial organizations: he arranged his £6,000 graduate loan via the bank where he holds his £1,000 overdraft, but his credit card is held via a different provider.

Next, know your enemies' terms of engagement. This is debt war after all, and we want a swift campaign of attack. At the moment, only the graduate loan has to be paid off within a fixed period. As long as the overdraft does not exceed its limit, the bank is happy to continue to add to the debt at the rate of 15 per cent each year.

Likewise, the credit card company loves increasing Luke's borrowings by 20 per cent a year, so long as he keeps paying off a minimal amount each month. This is how banks and all similar lenders make money. As long as they think you are good for the money in the long run, they will be happy to keep adding to the amount you owe by charging exorbitant rates of interest. They just sit back and tot up the sums.

BEWARE. This is why you should never just pay off the minimum monthly amount stipulated on your credit card statement. It is calculated to keep you locked in debt and the credit card company rolling in cash.

Sometimes this minimum amount can be as low as 2 per cent of the total balance. If your rate of borrowing is above 20 per cent on the card, it will take you a very long time to repay the total debt if you only pay off this minimum amount.

So Luke can effectively separate his debt into two levels: the low-rated long-term borrowings from his parents and the student loan company, and the high-rated short-term debts from financial institutions. What should he pay off first?

You might assume that since the debts to the Government (the student loan) and his parents are currently far larger than the other bits and bobs outstanding to the bank, he should try and reduce these first of all. After all, he can handle the smaller amounts pretty easily at present.

Let's compare them and see how much each debt grows over five years, assuming a constant 2 per cent annual inflation rate. Also, for the sake of comparison, assume the graduate loan is not paid off over a fixed period and Luke's salary remains below £20,000 (hard to believe for a lawyer I know, but imagine he's doing low-paid legal aid work).

DEBT TYPE	INTEREST RATE P.A	AMOUNT IN £ OVER 5 YEARS						AFTER 10 YEARS
		2000	2001	2002	2003	2004	2005	2010
Student loan	2%	5,000	5,100	5,202	5,306	5,412	5,520	6,095
Parental loan	nil	2,000	2,000	2,000	2,000	2,000	2,000	2,000
Graduate loan	10%	1,000	1,100	1,210	1,331	1,464	1,611	2,594

Overdraft	15%	1,000	1,150	1,323	1,521	1,749	2,011	4,046
Credit card debt	20%	1,000	1,200	1,440	1,728	2,074	2,488	6,192
Total		10,000	10,550	11,175	11,886	12,699	13,630	20,927
Interest rate			5.5%	5.9%	6.4%	6.8%	7.3%	

Striking, *n'est-ce pas?*

Look, in particular, at the jumping nature of credit card debt. After ten years, if left totally untended, the initial £1,000 credit card debt would balloon to £6,192. The £5,000 student loan, on the other hand, would grow at the rate of inflation to just £6,095.

So within ten years debt A, which began at a fifth of the size of debt B, can swell to enormous proportions and overtake debt B, which was initially five times larger. This is all because at a rate of 2 per cent, the larger (student loan) debt grows ten times slower than the smaller (credit card) one at 20 per cent.

The parental loan stays the same size, shrinking at an effective rate of 2 per cent each year, in line with inflation. But the debts to financial institutions, although each was half the size of this £2,000 parental loan to start with, all easily outstrip it after ten years. The total debt has more than doubled – it has gone up 109 per cent, and the interest alone of £10,927 is now more than the original debt of £10,000! Compare this with inflation over the ten-year period, which only went up 22 per cent in all. Only £2,200 would have accrued on the £10,000.

Notice also how the total debt starts to increase at a quicker pace, from 5.5 per cent in the first year to 7.3 per cent in the fifth, as the cycle continues and the higher-rated credit card borrowings make up proportionately more of the total outstanding amount.

Let's return to our original question: what debts should Luke try to clear first of all? The answer is, of course, those with financial institutions – particularly credit card borrowings, which can escalate at a frightening pace.

In 2000 the debts with low interest rates (the student and parental loans) made up 70 per cent of the total. Five years later they will make up 55 per cent of this amount. But after ten years, they will only account for 39 per cent of the debt mountain.

Graduate loans scams

OK, granted student *loans are a good thing: brilliant in fact. Compared to any other form of debt they are the best loans you can take out, ever, full stop. That's from a borrower's point of view of course. This is because they charge interest only at or around the current rate of inflation (about 2 per cent). So these debts should never overtake your earnings. This makes them very easy to control.*

Also, until you reach average earnings, or a sum near that level, you do not have to pay them off at all. What a bonus! If all your life you never get to this elevated salary position, you will never have to pay off the debt. And average earnings are growing ever faster, because the higher paid earn comparatively more than most other people.

Unfortunately, as the amount you can borrow from the Student Loans Company is now increasing (up to roughly £4,000 each academic year from 1999 onwards), in future you will have to start repayments when your salary goes above even £10,000. Nevertheless you should still put student loans on the back burner. Don't treat them like other debts. No, no, they are revered loans, which should not be lumped with other lesser animals. They are different and deservedly so.

On the other hand Graduate *loans, offered by Wise banks and not the Government once you have picked up your degree and entered the big wide world, can be dangerous and must be looked at warily.*

Graduation can be a costly business. Starting a new job with its attendant costs can prove even more expensive. Having finished university laden with debts, you may find the prospect of finding a deposit for a rented flat, buying suits and sundry other work gear as well as leaving the shelter of student accommodation rather daunting. At this most vulnerable of stages the banks will pop up like fairy godmothers to offer 'kind' assistance.

But watch out – they will be even more willing to help increase your debts by lending you more money, thus loading you with further debts. And being Fools we know why, don't we? So they get more revenue eventually, and tie you to them.

So be Foolish before diving in, and check their particular rates of lending. If the interest rate is genuinely lower than your other outstanding debts, then consider taking out the loan to pay off higher-rated debt, such as your credit card bill. This would help matters. But don't use the extra loan to allow yourself to spend even more and stave off repaying existing debts. Also, if you are considering the loan to make a major purchase, consider alternatives – check out the next chapter on gleaning cash.

To take on more debt willy-nilly may not prove the best policy in the long run. But if it reduces your overall debt by paying off more highly-rated loans, then by all means consider this route.

Lessons from Luke

So when looking at your debt position, look forward a few years and not at the present situation. This will give you an idea of how drastic things might become if not looked after immediately. In order to do this, the most important figure to consider is the interest rate. This shows the pace at which your debts will grow. This is a vital statistic, because as we have discovered above, the higher the rate, the quicker the growth.

Highly rated debts, such as credit card debts with interest rates as high as 20 per cent per year, are plants growing in a hothouse atmosphere. If not nipped in the bud, they will transform into huge alien triffids, engulf the rest of the greenhouse, and affect the management of the whole financial garden. And remember, chopping off the minimum amount each month will not be enough to kill the debt quickly. This is the amount the credit card company *wants* you to pay. So upset them by paying it all off as soon as possible!

Loans with lower rates, such as student loans at 2 per cent, are hardy perennials, growing a tiny bit each year in a mature flowerbed outside. These need little care and attention.

Overdrafts, normally in between these two extremes with a rate of about 10 per cent, tend to grow quite quickly on heavily composted and fertilized soil in the vegetable patch. Keep a careful eye on them to make sure they don't get out of control.

Rank your debts with the most expensive first. In order, this is the heated greenhouse (containing credit card debt), followed by the fertilized vegetable patch (nurturing borrowings from other banks) then the untended mature border (where low interest loans from parents, the Government and others live). You want to close down the costly greenhouse as soon as possible, transfer your debt plants to the vegetable patch at first, then gradually switch them to the low maintenance flowerbeds. This will free up the other areas of your financial garden for nurturing investments rather than debts over the long term.

For Emergency Use Only

If you are really up to your neck in debts and feel you are in serious danger of drowning, don't despair – there is drastic action you can take. Consult some Government statutory bodies and charities, which may help you through this sticky patch.

*The Citizens Advice Bureau, contactable at **www.advice guide.org.uk** or on 020 7833 2181, may be of some use in negotiating with your creditors. There are other agencies that are also willing to help. Try the National Debtline on 0800 8084000, or the Consumer Credit Counselling Service on 0800 1381111. All three organizations offer free advice and help in negotiating with creditors.*

Be very wary of letting yourself be declared bankrupt though. If you do so, you will relinquish all control to a myriad of Wise advisers, who will expensively decide amongst themselves how best to get their money back. Only once they have decided how to do this and implemented their ghastly plans will you be able to start your investment life.

And in the future you will probably be unable to get credit for any further borrowing. This could be a good thing, if you have an uncontrollable spending problem and find it impossible to stop forking out at every second opportunity. But it might restrict your

lifestyle. For instance, you would find it difficult to ever buy a home,
as you would be unable to arrange a mortgage with any lender.

Before bankruptcy, seek advice from these Government agencies,
as for once it is free and worthwhile.

Cut out credit cards from your cabbage patch!

The first Foolish lesson must be to pay off credit card debts before
tending to any others. This is easier said than done. Because of the
vast rates of interest charged by these nasty bits of plastic, you can
find yourself struggling to pay just the minimum amount required
each month. This is particularly the case if, horror of horrors, you
have more than one of these flexible fiends! And as we have already
said, paying off the minimum amount will not solve your debt
problems at all. You must pay off the whole debt.

Take shopaholic Karen, a credit card queen, who has three
separate plastic accounts. The first is a card originally taken out via
her bank, on which she owes £1,500 at the standard rate of 24 per
cent each year.

This year Karen decided to go on holiday to the Budgerigar
Islands. She took a different card with her because it was accepted at
more places in the Budgerigars than her bank's card. Karen has just
returned after racking up a sizeable bill of £2,000, payable (thankfully)
at the comparatively knockdown rate of 12 per cent per year.

On top of this, Karen has built up a £1,000 balance on a charge
card she took out from a local department store, Sharks and
Mincers. When she first got the S&M card it seemed so handy. She
had to buy a wedding present for her sister and the card, with its
introductory offer of £25 free spending with her first purchase,
seemed ideal for the purpose.

However, since then lots of her friends have got married as
well. So, as presents have been bought and a few celebratory hen
lunches have been eaten in S&M's top floor restaurant, the
balance has mounted. And at the exorbitant annual interest rate of
36 per cent, the debt is rising rapidly.

So Karen owes, in total, £4,500 on her cards. What should she do to cut the burden? As we did with Luke, she should take the debts individually and rank them according to their rate of growth.

CARD	AMOUNT	INTEREST RATE P.A	MONTHLY INCREASE
Budgie Holiday	2,000	12%	1% or £20
Karen's Bank	1,500	24%	2% or £30
S&M Store	1,000	36%	3% or £30
Total	4,500		£85

Which balance should Karen chop out first of all? How should she pay off her debts, noting that each card provider requires her to pay £10 minimum per month?

First look at Karen's own (incoming) cash situation. At the moment she can only afford to pay off £100 per month. Then look at the table above. The debts on the S&M store card are growing three times faster than those on the card she took to the Budgerigars.

If she split the £100 repayment between all three card providers, the £33 to S&M would only just cover the amount the £1,000 balance grew last month, £30. Thus she should try to pay off this fast-growing animal before tackling the others. In the first month, the Bank and Budgie should both receive the £10 minimum repayment, and the remaining £80 should go to S&M. You might have thought that she should try and tackle the largest debt, to Budgie. But this is growing a third more slowly than the S&M debt. Leave the S&M untended and the amount will soon swamp the other two outstanding amounts.

Think of debt maintenance as putting out a fire. Attack the most rapidly spreading area first, whilst containing the most easily manageable outbreak. Once the worst fire is under control, go and tend to the other flames in your debt portfolio.

Credit cards are the most combustible forms of debt because, out of control, they can set fire to the rest of your financial structure. Plan your whole financial life around them and you are building your funeral pyre, forever playing one fire off against another. But remember, fire-fighting is a dangerous profession. And fire-eating is an illusion! Instead of a funeral pyre you want to build a sturdy fiscal pillar. Make a good start by cancelling out those combustible credit card debts first of all!

If, the following month, Karen has £500 left over to pay off her debts, she should do the same thing and concentrate on the S&M Store card. Last month she reduced her S&M debt to £950 by repaying £50 in addition to the £30 interest. This outstanding balance attracted £28.50 interest, so £978.50 was still owed in all.

Assuming that the minimum £10 repayment is again made to the other two card providers, this leaves Karen with £480 to throw at the S&M debt. This cuts it to a much more manageable £498.50. Over these two months, the Budgie balance will only have risen by £20, or roughly 1 per cent.

Once the S&M balance has been cleared, the next quickest growing balance, Karen's bank's card with a rate of 24 per cent (double that of the Budgie card), should be tackled in a similar manner.

Short cuts to containment

However, you might think all this methodical repayment quite a long-winded process. You'll be glad to hear that there are a number of short cuts you might try, but the most important step is to understand your particular situation before attempting to put them into practice. Once you're *au fait* with your debt, it will seem easier to tackle these tips and thus take the Wise and their confusing tricks head-on.

With your Foolish thinking cap on, you know that the lower the interest rate, the slower a debt will grow. Naturally, therefore, you want to make all your debts liable for as low a level of interest as possible.

From now on, if you must have a credit card for, say, emergency purchases abroad, always use one with the lowest possible rate of interest. Never use ones that charge you a fee just to hold the card in your wallet each year.

Also, be mercenary with your cards. Just as Wise financial providers of credit cards subject their victims to the long-term torture of high interest rate charges, so you can strike back with short stabs. *Never be loyal to your lenders.*

Karen admitted the S&M Store card's introductory offer was great – £25 off her first purchase. Fine, take up this offer, use it for that first bargain purchase, pay off the debt promptly so it incurs as little interest as possible – then cut up S&M's card so that you can never, ever, use it again!

Karen was being supremely Foolish when she chose to take a card other than her bank's card to the Budgerigars. This wasn't because it was more widely accepted in the Budgies. No, it was because its annual interest rate at 12 per cent was half that of her bank's card, which charges 24 per cent.

This begs the question why Karen keeps any of her borrowings on the bank's card, and doesn't transfer them to the Budgie card. I'm sure Budgie bank will be keen to let her transfer her borrowings to their fledgling operation. In that way they hope to make more money by charging interest on a bigger balance.

Karen's bank might be fine for clearing cheques and running current accounts, but that doesn't necessarily mean it provides good value for customers across all its services, including its credit cards. You might be a victim but there's no need to be a captive. So, shop your debt around. That's right, ring up the Budgie card's head office and ask to move your debt to them.

The number of credit card providers in the UK has leapt lately. You can now choose between seventy of the little devils. That doesn't include their gold and platinum versions either. All are desperate to build up business. No doubt if you have one card, you have found many 'exclusive' invitations to take out cards cluttering up your doormat of a morning. Some offer attractively low rates of interest to entice you to swap your outstanding balance.

This can be a good Foolish thing to do. But be careful that the introductory interest rate doesn't leap up unannounced soon afterwards. (You could also apply for a card on the Internet, many of which are very cheap because electronic transactions cost less. Look at the Prudential's Egg card, for example, at **www.egg.com**.)

And don't worry about some cards being more acceptable in certain outlets than others. Most credit cards divide into Visas and Mastercards. Most outlets take both, don't they? And if they don't, then don't fret, be Foolish, because you are saving money already. However, if you must buy this particular item, go and shop elsewhere.

Shopping your debt around might prove harder with high-interest charging cards. Take, for example, S&M's store card, which seduced Karen before she learnt about disloyalty. Many stores are unwilling to let go of their customers' debts. After all, the purpose of the card was to keep punters enthralled in the first place and coming back for more purchases. In such an instance, concentrate all your resources on paying off this debt. More tips on how to do this follow in the next section.

Finally, before we kiss goodbye to those beastly credit cards, if you still want an emergency flexible fiend, make sure you only use it in an emergency and not on impulse. And check it attracts no annual administrative fee. Ideally, try to find a card that offers an interest-free period between the purchase date and the statement date. That way, you will be able to stab the Wise provider again – if you pay off the emergency purchase in full immediately, it will not incur any interest whatsoever. You will have effectively benefited by gaining credit without being charged for it.

And whatever you do, don't just pay off the minimum amount each month. This is designed to keep you in debt and the credit company in cash. Last year the total amount of credit card debt owed by Britons jumped 14 per cent to £109 billion! 16.5 million people in the UK have some form of unsecured borrowing, such as credit card debt. That makes the average debt £6,362 per person. Clear this and you've cracked a significant problem and turned the corner towards Foolishness.

Other debt

OK, so you've got your credit cards under control but still have substantial debts to worry about. Let's look at Luke's situation again.

You remember he had low-interest debts of £7,000 (student loans and parental loans), but £3,000 in fast-growing high-interest debts with various financial providers. These comprised a £1,000 overdraft at 15 per cent, £1,000 credit card borrowings at 20 per cent, and £1,000 outstanding from a graduate loan charging 10 per cent with a fixed repayment term monthly.

Now we know he should pay off the credit card debt first, since it is growing fastest. However, there might be a short cut. Notice how the graduate loan charges the lowest rate of interest – half that on the credit card. This is partly because it is being repaid over a fixed term, so the finance company knows it will receive payments regularly.

Luke might, in a Foolish spirit, try to convert all his high-interest debt to this low level rate or thereabouts. He might be able to go to the loan provider, knowing that he can afford to pay off a fixed sum of £100 a month by direct debit, and ask at what rate they would be prepared to take on the other £2,000 worth of debts. If he only managed to negotiate a total rate of 12.5 per cent, this would still be better than his previous arrangement, with £1,000 owed at 15 per cent and another £1,000 at 20 per cent. In fact, it is over a quarter cheaper.

Similarly, Karen could have gone to her bank or the Budgie bank to try to borrow enough to pay off her outstanding S&M balance. This was growing at 36 per cent per year. So any rate less than that would have been an improvement.

Normally, the bank that has your current account will be the most amenable to such debt shopping and transferral. But this is not always the case. As always, check the rates on their personal loans and compare them to those on your current debts.

Remember, banks want you to be in debt – that's how they earn their money, from your interest payments. So don't be scared of the bank manager – you're helping him as much as he's helping you. It's a business arrangement. He'll almost welcome you with open arms. The cheapest debts of all are mortgages, because they are secured by the value of your house. However, that is best left for later on in Chapter Four.

Don't be loyal to your bank, either. There is nothing stopping you switching your current account to a rival bank if you think they will offer a lower interest rate. A debt should be for as short a period as possible, so if paying it off by direct debit makes its life shorter and less painful then switch. Euthanasia for debts is a good thing!

The discipline of paying off interest on a regular basis will also stand you in good stead to start investing. If you know how much you have to save, and what return you have to make to satisfy your long-term investment goals, then you can start saving regularly once the debt is paid off.

How managing debts can help your investments: the miracle of compounding returns

Earlier in this chapter we showed how Luke's initial debt of £10,000 could more than double to £20,927 over ten years if left alone and untended. This means the debt would have grown by an average of 7.66 per cent per year. Now imagine if it was left alone for a further twenty years. How much would Luke owe by then? The answer is a staggering £91,544. That is quite a remarkable rate of growth. It represents a total increase of 815 per cent on the original debt.

Now reverse the picture and imagine instead that you have been left £10,000 by a doting grandmother. Say you put this in a savings account, which guarantees an interest rate of 7.66 per cent a year (the same as the growth rate of the debt discussed above). Your cash pile would thus grow to £91,544 after thirty years, without you lifting a finger – a total return of 815 per cent. Not bad eh?

This is the magic of compounding returns, which we briefly touched on in the opening sequence. As long as no deposits are withdrawn during this period, quite small amounts of money will grow to become significant sums. The money grows at a compounded, or increasing, rate of interest, as the amount on which interest is charged gets larger.

Now not everybody has a lump sum to lock away. But the same principle applies if you can salt away a little each month, as long as you keep the cash there and contribute regularly. For example, someone putting just £100 aside each month in an account paying 7.66 per cent interest a year will see this become £18,416 after ten years. Pretty tidy! The total amount invested would be £100 (the amount invested monthly) times the 120 months (the number of months in ten years). This adds up to £12,000. The amount made in interest over this period is thus £6,416, representing a total return of 53.5 per cent.

But the really amazing thing is that over a longer period of time, as this sum continues to build by £100 each month and is supplemented by 7.66 per cent of the total at the end of each year, the total return improves significantly. After twenty years you would have £56,474 in total. That makes a return of 134 per cent from the £24,000 invested, despite a constant annual interest rate of 7.66 per cent. Over thirty years the sum would grow to £139,141. After forty years it would be £320,187 and after fifty years, an incredible £707,823.

There is a quite complicated formula that can calculate such returns from regular monthly investments, given a constant interest rate. However, we don't want to bother you with such mathematical conundrums. Instead you can go to a page on the *Motley Fool's* American site that will calculate these sums for you if you plug in the relevant data.

For working out compounding returns try the Foolish savings calculator: **www.calcbuilder.com/cgi-bin/calcs/SAV2.cgi/themotleyfool**. Or if you get lost, revert to the general index of Foolish calculators at **www.fool.com/calcs/calculators.htm.**

By calculating predicted returns using the formulas on these calculators, you will also be able to compare various savings and investment products easily, which is a good Foolish habit. By doing this you can become as knowledgeable as the Wisest adviser.

Use any savings to pay off your debts

So, when it comes to sorting out your financial affairs, the miracle of compounding means that time is on your side. However, the start is still crucial. Let us go back to the analogy about running a marathon. To run such a long race you want to be as prepared as possible. That means being as unencumbered by debts as you can. Remember, you should not be saving while paying off high-interest loans.

Banks and other financial institutions aim to lend out money at a higher interest rate than the rate they pay on deposits lodged with them. This is how they make their money. Thus, if you try to save while paying off debts, you will be unable to make much head speed and will indeed fall behind plain exhausted trying to pay off your debt. The debt will take longer to disappear, and your savings will grow more slowly, as you cannot afford to devote all resources to building them up. Far better to concentrate all available resources on stamping out the debt before starting to save and invest at all. It might take a year or so, but you will still have plenty of profitable time left to invest in.

If you already have some savings, say £1,000, growing at 5 per cent per year, but also have total debts of £2,000, which are larger than the savings pot and growing at 10 per cent per year, your debt is growing at double the rate of your savings. If left untended the debt will soon spiral out of control and the savings will seem insignificant in comparison. It would be far better in this circumstance to use the small amount of savings to pay off the debt so that it falls more quickly.

Take Jerry and Carl. Both want to save regular sums from their monthly income over ten years. Both have £200 to spare each month, or £1,200 per year. But both also have debts of £2,000. These grow by 20 per cent a year.

Jerry decides to put £100 aside each month in a savings account, which pays 5 per cent interest annually. The other £100 goes on paying off a little bit of the debt. He only starts putting the full £200 in the savings account once he has paid off his debt.

Meanwhile Carl calmly reckons he will concentrate on killing the debt first of all and pays the £200 each month to his lenders, before attempting to start saving in the same savings account as Jerry. But he will put in the full £200 from the beginning of his saving period.

Who will be better off with their savings plan after ten years? Assume that the interest on both debts and savings is calculated on an annual basis.

YEAR	2000	2001	2002	2003	2004	2005	2010
Jerry (debts)	-2,000	-1,200	-240	nil	nil	nil	nil
(savings)	nil	1,260	2,583	4,917	7,683	10,587	27,437
(total)	-2,000	60	2,343				
Carl (debts)	-2,000	nil	nil	nil	nil	nil	nil
(savings)	nil	nil	2,520	5,166	7,944	10,862	27,787
(total)	-2,000	nil	2,520				

Jerry may have started to save earlier than Carl, but Carl is the first to be able to devote all his surplus monthly reserves to the savings plan, a clear fifteen months ahead of Jerry. Thus after only two years of the plan he is ahead of Jerry overall, even though Jerry started saving half his monthly surplus, or £100, a year before Carl started saving at all.

Because the 5 per cent interest rate used in this example is so tiny, the sums are not significantly different after the ten-year period. But remember, Jerry will never catch up with Carl because of his debt mismanagement at the beginning.

And if Carl had chosen to invest his money elsewhere in a vehicle that gave a higher return of say 10 per cent, then the discrepancies would have been more marked after ten years. More about such wonderful things with great returns can be found later on in this book.

Having read this far, we have hopefully cleared up your debts or at least shown you how this task should be accomplished. Perhaps you have even used what little savings you had tucked away to do this. Hmmm. You may now be wondering where the cash you had earmarked to invest is going to come from!

Well let's move a step further down the Foolish pathway and

look at this elusive element in the investment equation: cash. Come, let's go cash gleaning!

A Foolish footnote on hire purchase schemes

We haven't covered these common beasts yet, but be careful when you encounter them because they can be very viperous. Sure you want a video player and the latest television. And £10 a week for a year may not seem like much to get hold of them.

But that payment soon tots up. If you had waited patiently you would have been able to buy the TV outright within a few months! The price of electrical goods sold in this way is declining all the time. You might be able to save a little each week from elsewhere, or perhaps borrow more effectively from another source in order to buy the video outright.

Perhaps you want a car at '0 per cent finance' (sic) as well. But check out the hidden terms on these purchases very carefully. You might soon find you can finance the purchase using other means. Alternative schemes might work out cheaper.

Ten Foolish steps out of debt

1. Debts can destroy any savings you have, since banks ensure debts grow more rapidly than cash on deposit.
2. Credit cards are particularly vicious beasts. Debts on them grow the quickest. Cut them out as soon as you can. If you use them to make a purchase, pay off the debt in full when you get the statement.
3. Work out the interest rates charged on your various debts. This shows the rate at which the debt grows.
4. Negotiate to convert these outstanding debts to the lowest rate.
5. Pay off debts before beginning to invest.
6. Treat student loans separately. Don't rush to pay them off, since the interest rate charged is very low.
7. Beware of graduate loans and other personal borrowing arrangements. Check their interest rates.

8. The miracle of compounding returns means regular savings can grow into substantial amounts.
9. Use any savings you have to pay off your debts more quickly.
10. Avoid hire purchase schemes.

Chapter Two – Cash in hand

Money talks . . . but all mine ever says is goodbye.
Anonymous

OK. Now you know why you should clear your debts before investing. But how on earth are you going to scrape the money together to do this? How do you get yourself into a position to take this vital first step along the financial path to investing Foolishly?

You could hope for a windfall from somewhere. Perhaps you reckon you deserve a salary rise. Maybe your building society will magically become a bank and give you some shares. An aged fairy godmother might leave you some crumbs in her will. Or possibly one day you will check your current account balance and find you have been mistakenly credited with an extra £1,000. But all these pipe dreams are merely that: wishes and wild speculations, which unfortunately are unlikely to come true.

Coming back down to earth, with your Foolish eyes fixed firmly on the ground again, you may think you have little spare cash to set aside each month after you have paid off your bills and kept the wolf from the door. However, we all have more than we think. It's just that most of us are all too human as well. We find it far too easy to spend the hard-earned money we have in our hands.

Let's face it, you probably sneak off to the pictures a few times each month before you even start to consider your bills. Few of us account for the niceties of life. Do you really need that delicious tall cappuccino with extra cream and cinnamon every morning? Perhaps Monday is the only working day that really deserves such a treat. There are many ways, practical and frankly ridiculous, of gleaning cash. Everyone has their own particular method of saving a bit here or there.

My own concerns sightseeing in London. Go to Baker Street on any morning during the summer and you will see hordes of tourists piling into Madame Tussauds. Gaggles of tour bus operators gather outside the exit of the waxworks, eager to get unsuspecting tourists to go on their costly excursions around the capital. These can cost as much as £10 a head. But you don't have to do this unless you particularly want to listen to some static-ridden recorded description of the Telecom tower's construction.

No, instead of forking out a tenner, hop on an authentic red Routemaster London bus. The number 11 is particularly suitable. You can find it near Victoria station. Its route passes Westminster Abbey and the Houses of Parliament before proceeding up Whitehall to Trafalgar Square, then along the Strand and Fleet Street towards a glorious view of St Paul's Cathedral from the other side of Ludgate Hill. The trip ends near the Bank of England. All this for £1 per adult, and no inaudible commentary thrown in either.

Now that's off my chest and before the tour operators come marching down Baker Street to the Fool's UK HQ, I'd better start with some more conventional methods of saving money, which might be of more use if you're not planning to visit London this year.

Living below your means

One of the most popular of the 500 or so message boards on the Motley Fool Web site (**www.fool.co.uk**) has the grand title of *Living Below Your Means*. It has been aptly dubbed the 'frugal' board by the many individual Fools who have posted thousands of messages there (**boards.fool.co.uk**). Each has contributed particular hints on how to scrimp and save. Much of their Foolish advice is included in this chapter, and for this I am hugely indebted.

Saving can be a lonely business. It may mean you can no longer afford to do all the things you would ideally like to. Fewer cinema trips, not so many restaurant meals, cheaper holidays to less exotic destinations: all these economies may have to be made. But knowing there are others going through the same belt-tightening process makes it easier to bear if you are used to spending freely and easily. Swapping stories with those further along the investment track can reassure you that this short-term pain is worth all the effort in the long run.

In any case, saving money does not necessarily have to involve painful restrictions on the things you enjoy doing. Most people's income goes on the essential costs of living, rather than frivolous luxuries. So by making economies in your essential costs, you may still be able to enjoy the little things in life. The road to investment doesn't have to resemble a treadmill.

Of course, if you truly want to invest Foolishly you are going to have to get some cash together somehow, first to pay off your outstanding debts, then to start investing regularly each month. But this task doesn't have to be shrouded in Dickensian gloom if you follow certain Foolish principles.

Nevertheless, this master of tragic Victorian novel-writing is rather good at illustrating some grim but pertinent points. In *David Copperfield* he introduces his loyal readers to a Mr Micawber, who famously intones, 'Annual income twenty pounds, annual expenditure nineteen nineteen and six, result happiness. Annual income twenty pounds, annual expenditure twenty pounds ought and six, result misery ...'

The essential point is this: if your monthly income is less than your total monthly outgoings you will be unhappy in the long run. However, if you can turn this position around so that you have some surplus each month, then you will become happier. Now go, Mr Micawber, thanks for the moral lesson, but let's sort this out Foolishly.

Assume first of all that your income is constant, as in Mr Micawber's case. This will focus our efforts on expenditure, which seems to fluctuate more and is easier for most of us to control. We will look at boosting income in the next chapter.

Essential spending vs. luxurious living

Every Wise financial book under the sun recommends doing a budget, but I fear humans aren't as rigid as all that. Say your cousin from Australia comes over to visit suddenly. What do you do if she wants to go out to a top show in London's West End while she's in town? Do you say, 'Sorry, I have only allocated £20 to evening excursions each month, and the £10 meal I had in Pizza Express last Friday takes me over my limit, so I'll have to say no, not this time. If you're around again next month we might consider *Cats*. Enjoy the show if you go.'?

No of course you don't, you old skinflint. She's a cousin from the other side of the world and you only see her once in a blue moon. You might as well enjoy her company whilst you can. Life isn't that long, and there's not much point living if you can't enjoy yourself once in a while. (On the other hand, if your cousin is a bit of a family black sheep and you can't stand Andrew Lloyd-Webber, you have a perfect excuse not to attend!)

It is a much better bet to adopt some broad guidelines. This is far preferable to berating yourself when you almost inevitably fail to stick to strict and unrealistic monthly budgets. And when sketching out these guidelines, you should allow yourself to live a little – not that you probably need much encouragement – by incorporating some flexibility into your cash-gleaning plans.

But a Foolish first must be to divide your annual outgoings into 'essential' expenses and 'naughty but nice' luxuries. The great thing about luxuries is that they are luxurious precisely because they are unpredictable, out of the ordinary, and change all the time according to your whims. Variety is the spice of life, and there is no need to cut down your luxuries and detail exactly what these surprises are, as long as your essential expenditure is under control and is pared down as far as possible.

If you Foolishly account for this element of surprise, you won't be worrying about the Wise men after your money when a luxury comes up that you can't afford, but also can't bear to throw away. Luxuries are things you decide about.

Essentials, on the other hand, are items that you really can't live without. OK, you might say, we all know what our luxuries are – they are the nice things in life, the treats that make life worth living, and at the end of the day you can turn them down and still survive. But what exactly are essentials? If we're really honest, these are the ultimate basics of food, warmth and shelter.

If you took away one or other of these essentials then investing would probably be the last thing on your mind. There's no getting around it – you have to spend money on these items to sustain yourself. If you have others to support then, naturally, you must factor in the cost of looking after these loved ones as well.

Work out how much you spend on clothing yourself, feeding yourself, accommodation costs, utility and household bills for such essentials as water, power (heating and light) and cleaning costs; and don't forget the Council Tax. Account for those you have to support in your reckoning.

There are other bare necessities as well. Most people have to travel to work. Include such transport costs in this essential list along with other travel expenses, such as the trip to the local supermarket. However, any other non-essential travel costs should be considered luxuries.

Communication also costs money. Most people probably regard the telephone as a necessary part of modern living, but it is easy to be luxurious when using it. When you have a land line, a mobile, an answerphone service and an expensive modem connection to the Internet, these costs soon mount up. At the Fool, we think of the Internet as a pretty useful tool for living nowadays, so we shall say a telephone line (probably a fixed one for now) is pretty essential. But then we are biased!

Maybe spending on toiletries, personal hygiene, cleaning and bedding should also be included under basic shopping costs.

So the basic essentials of modern living are:

Accommodation;
Household bills – power (heating and light), water, Council Tax, cleaning and bedding costs;

Travel expenses;
Food;
Clothing;
Telephone connection of some sort.

All the rest are luxuries of one description or other. I hope this doesn't sound too bleak in a millennial-cum-apocalyptic way! Perhaps those of more Puritan tastes reckon I'm overdoing it on the essentials already.

Now you know you have to spend money on these somehow. So work out how you can cut costs here. Below I have taken each essential item in turn and offered some tips on frugal living, garnered from many sources including the Fool's message boards.

Accommodation

Finding a suitably Foolish place to live opens a whole can of worms, which deserves a complete volume outlining the various Wise pits that unsuspecting Fools can fall into. Chapter Four will deal with the specific pros and cons of renting somewhere to live against buying a place. For now, let us just admit that for most people this is the most immutable aspect of their finances: the thing you find hardest to change.

Sure, you can move. But it is not as easy as it sounds to up sticks and plant yourself somewhere else. Particularly as you have to find that 'somewhere else' first. This juggling act is very hard to perform smoothly. It is far easier to stop spending on something else, renegotiate a debt or maybe arrange a new method of bill payment. To try to sell a property, or end a lease earlier than planned, is harder to accomplish than either of these, and a lot more stressful.

Whether you are moving out of your present place or moving into your new abode, you are relying on other people to comply with your Foolish wishes. You cannot simply enact your decisions immediately, which you can do if you decide to pay a bill differently, or switch your telecom connection to a new telephone company. The costs of accommodation are thus fixed for most people, at least in the short term and as long as interest rates don't move massively.

Over a longer period it is quite possible to arrange accommodation that doesn't create as large a dent in your income, but this needs careful planning, particularly as it is such a dominant aspect of most people's financial picture. For more information, skip to Chapter Four.

Household bills

Do you find you just cannot keep track of bills? Do you develop a sinking feeling of surprise mixed with alarm when the little brown envelopes come through the letterbox and land on your doormat with a depressing thud? Does that sound knock you sideways? As a Fool you should not be fearful. You should be in control, keep bills organized and take them in your stride.

Since you know you have these essential expenses to pay, you should deal with them first, at the beginning of the month or whenever you are paid. This is far better than letting them build up and then paying them off at the last minute in a desperate scramble.

Some you can do very little about. Council Tax, determined by the value of the house you live in, just has to be faced and paid. If you know it's coming then why not just put it on monthly direct debit and forget about it? This spirits away the sum you owe before you can spend it on more luxurious things.

The privatization of the utilities by the Conservative government during the 1980s and 90s was meant to open up a new era of choice and better service for the consumer. In olden times, before the reign of Margaret Thatcher, the state owned these vital industries. Thus you had one national price for water, gas and electricity, set by the Water, Gas and Electricity Boards respectively, just as sending a letter first class still costs the same across the country. By selling off these various utility industries in different lumps and sizes, the state hoped to encourage competition for customers between the newly private companies, thus either bringing consumer costs down or service standards up. This golden prospect has come to pass more quickly in some industries than others.

For instance I think you are pretty much stuck with the water supplier you have. There is little you can do to get cheaper water. Some companies have a metered system but most merely charge a flat rate. So most water-saving techniques may be redundant, unless of course, like a good citizen of the planet, you feel the urge to conserve resources in an effort to combat the threats of global warming. (However, do remember that most tap water is perfectly safe to drink, despite the scare stories that frequently crop up in the press. Don't be put off. It's not as if Britain is a developing country with sewerage problems. So dispense with over-priced bottled water. Milk, and in some cases beer, are cheaper than water in plastic bottles! If you're still worried, why not get a cheap water filter system?)

However, back to our original point. Since water rates are something you're stuck with, why not pay them by direct debit, like the Council Tax, and have done with them?

When it comes to gas and electricity, the modern deregulated landscape is significantly different from when the gas-man and the electricity board assumed disproportionately important roles in people's lives. You may not have noticed, but power providers are out there begging for your custom. Have you wondered why British Gas split to become BG and Centrica? It was so it would not just be thought of as an old-style integrated gas company, but two new singing and dancing power providers.

If you have traditionally used gas to heat your house and cook your food, and electricity to run other appliances, then look at the alternatives. Many power companies are willing to provide central heating (whether it is run on gas or oil) and electricity together, so that you get one bill: easy and in many cases cheaper than previous arrangements. To discover the most economic and Foolish ways to obtain electricity and gas, it is worth looking at a Web site called **www.buy.co.uk**. This site asks a few questions about how you use these utilities, then compares rates and the various options open to you. As with the other bills, paying a fixed proportion of your bill each month by direct debit will stop you from spending the money on luxuries.

Power saving tips are numerous. Here is just one example: never use a tumble dryer. Let your clothes dry naturally in an airing cupboard or on a radiator. Next time you are tempted to switch on a tumble dryer, look at the electricity meter. You will see how this appliance eats up energy like nobody's business, sending the meter whirring around. Look on the Fool's *Living Below Your Means* board for further frugal power saving tips.

Some people advocate delaying payment of household bills until the last possible date given on those nasty red final demands. That way, you can use your money how you wish before having to confront your bills. However, don't be deluded by this sense of freedom. These bills have to be paid sometime. Better to clear them first of all, so you know exactly what funds remain until you receive your next batch of income.

Travel

One of the quickest ways to lose money is to own and run a motor car. A recent study worked out that if you buy a new car, within only a year in some cases (in which it has covered 10,000 miles on average) the same vehicle will only fetch half the price that you initially paid for it. Simply driving a car away from the salesroom takes a quarter of its value away in one fell swoop. It is now a 'used' vehicle.

Only certain resilient German cars would be worth over half their purchase price after two years. Few things lose their value so quickly. Houses don't drop in price quite like that. Paintings keep their value. Overall, the largest blue chip shares have withstood long-term pressures and appreciated quite significantly (more later on this in part two of this book).

If you are still keen on buying a new car, work out, on top of this depreciation, how expensive it will be to run. Include insurance, road tax, maintenance and servicing, and of course heavily taxed fuel, which forever seems to be rising in price.

All in all cars are very expensive to own, but they should be an easy habit to kick. Ask yourself how often you use the rusting set of wheels. Do you really need it to get to work? Is public transport a viable alternative? Could you get your shopping delivered to your home? Many chains offer this service. It is a much better method of getting household provisions than trudging to the supermarket each week.

Have you considered cycling to get around instead? Or walking? They are also superb ways to see cities, rather than being snarled up in traffic. And in some cases they can prove quicker and less stressful than travelling by car in an area you don't know.

But if, like Mr Toad in *The Wind in the Willows*, you are a committed car addict, dedicated to the romantic independence of the open road, you should at least try to curb your excesses. Because of the way they rapidly depreciate, never buy a new car. Second-hand vehicles, from registered dealers, offer a much better bargain.

If you must have the latest model, consider buying it on the continent, where cars are cheaper. If you spend exorbitant amounts of money on a car, perhaps you should consider attributing a certain proportion, the amount which exceeds your vital needs, to the realms of luxurious rather than essential spending.

If you can commute to work via public transport and only use a car at the weekend, you could dispense with the car altogether and maybe rent one for specific trips away. I bet if you did this and bought an annual railway season ticket, your total travel expenditure would be less than the costs of owning and running a car.

If you are an infrequent rail user, but still make a few journeys each month by train, it may still be worth buying a railcard. These are not just designed for the under twenty-fives and over sixty-fives. In certain rail operating regions, you can get Network cards for less than £20, offering a third off all off-peak rail fares.

Whilst on this subject, if you only use the Tube occasionally and only in central London, invest in a carnet of ten tickets. This costs £11, or £1.10 per ticket. Compare that with an extortionate £1.50 for an individual journey in central London. The carnet, which lasts one year, offers a 25 per cent reduction on each journey.

Again, if you spend more than the cheapest cost of the

journey to the office, you are eating into your luxurious spending zone. For example, say you have a thirty-mile daily commute, which is equally possible by car or train and takes the same amount of time by either method. Let's say the train journey costs £15 for a return ticket at peak times and your car eats up petrol at the rate of 20p per mile. Thus petrol for the daily journey costs £12.

Superficially, the car looks £3 cheaper to use each day. However, if you buy an annual season ticket, the cost of the train journey halves to £7.50 per day; whereas for the car, you have to add in how much the vehicle cost to purchase initially and how much it costs to run, including regular servicing charges, road tax and insurance. With all these accounted for at, say, £3 per day, the real price of the daily commute rises to £15 – double the daily cost of travelling to work by train.

Public transport, despite its drawbacks, is definitely Foolish.

Food

Hopefully there are fewer worms in this particular parcel! During the past twenty years, any observant Fool can hardly fail to have noticed that British eating habits have undergone a complete overhaul. In the late 1970s, spaghetti bolognese was considered a delicacy that required careful preparation. When most people ate spaghetti they opened a tin of cooked pasta strands, already soaked in tomato sauce. These 'worms' were heated up and poured on to buttered toast. Go to any supermarket worth its salt nowadays and you can find freshly made pasta of all shapes and forms stacked neatly beside a huge spread of stir-in Italian-style pasta sauces, no doubt concocted somewhere in the Midlands. People's tastes have widened incredibly, so much so that the meat and two veg menu of yesteryear increasingly seems to be a threatened species, along with Sunday lunch, boiled cabbage and stew.

This taste transformation is mainly due to two trends. First, the explosion in popularity of the ready-made meal. Before the

1980s most people enjoyed a hot meal at work in the middle of the day, either in a subsidized staff canteen or in numerous chop-houses and cafes sited around offices. But in the 1980s, when work patterns changed and business was done around the clock, sales of sandwiches soared. The sandwich was convenient and cheap. You could eat it on the go or at your desk. This led to the demise of the midday meal as an institution. The British Sandwich Association reckons that 'some 80 per cent of workers eat sandwiches at least once a week during meal breaks at work, and more than 30 per cent eat them every day.' There are easily more McDonald's than chop-houses in London now, and certainly more fast-food burgers are devoured than plates of sausages and mash.

Changes in working habits are also partly responsible for the demise of home cooking. It is now common for both partners in a family to be out at work during the day, and no one has time to slave over the stove at home preparing a fresh meal each evening. It seems much more convenient to shove a ready-cooked meal in the oven instead, go out and grab a take-away pizza, or stay out and have a curry. This brings us to the second big trend in eating habits: the development of 'eating out' as a pastime.

What were restaurants like twenty years ago? Most were either attached to hotels or were very costly establishments, commonly with French menus and waiters in dickie bows like Manuel in *Fawlty Towers*. It was hardly surprising that so few people ate out! Since those dark days, though, the restaurant trade has been revolutionized. The food styles of many different countries, Italian, French, American, Mexican, Thai, Chinese, Indian and Moroccan can be found in most reasonably sized towns. *Time Out*, the London entertainment guide, recently classified nearly a hundred different styles of restaurants in the capital, including such outlandish types as Afghan, Burmese and Outer Mongolian (really? – Ed.). Quite extraordinary.

You may be wondering what exactly this gastronomic essay has to do with saving money. Well, in this flight to convenience food, many have forgotten how to cook at home. Have you noticed how many cooking programmes there are on television? Many are delivered with the hopeless novice in mind. *Can't*

Cook, Won't Cook and Delia Smith's *How to Cook* are just two examples, which no one would have dreamt of running in the 1960s. Dear Delia, as she is styled, has become a millionaire many times over on the back of this change of affairs.

But if you know how to cook cheaply, you can save yourself much money and still entertain and have fun with your friends. Now I'm not going to change this book into the *Fool's Guide to Food* – though with demand for cookery books being what it is, we'd better slap a trademark on that idea. But just consider how you can save money by rekindling this noble art.

Most people nowadays spend a fortune on convenience foods or eating out. Ask yourself how often you eat out. If it was twice last week, you are probably only counting the meals you had in restaurants. On top of this you must consider the number of take-away pizzas you ate, the sandwiches you wolfed down at your desk at lunchtime and the snacks in the pub at the weekend.

Tot up all this gorging and if you find you have spent more on convenience foods than on your weekly food shop, then you should easily be able to tighten your belt a little. Consider making your own sandwiches, or bringing the leftovers from the night before into the office the next day. Compound your cooking! Get more out of the meals you cook. On top of all this, if you cook more of your own food, you should become fitter as well as more Foolish.

Clothing

Some mad people enjoy shopping for clothes. Retailers convince them that it is a fun way to spend your time, a pastime. Personally, I've never thought of cash burning as a particularly enjoyable pursuit, but don't let me stop anybody. But if you shop for fun then consign that particular activity to the realms of luxury.

In this section we are dealing with essentials – things you need to get by. You will need certain clothes more than others, as your job dictates. If you work down the drains repairing sewers, you will need some pretty sturdy rubber boots and a steady supply of long lasting and extra thick clothes to protect you from the damp and cold of the underground tunnels. (Hopefully your job will provide much of the special clothing required.)

However, if you work in an office you probably have to wear a suit and look reasonably respectable, despite the recent relaxation of dress codes. It's unlikely your company will help you with this. So what should you do to fund this unwanted wardrobe of uncomfortable yet necessary clothing? Never buy as and when you need to, unless you're planning to resign and go travelling around the world before long. If you envisage sticking out the suit-style job for, say, the coming year, plan your clothes spending over that whole year.

When the sales are on, as they are almost year-round now except in the lead-up to Christmas, stock up your wardrobe with essentials like underwear and shirts at bargain prices, even if you don't necessarily need such items immediately. When you do desperately need such stuff it may be more expensive. Now I'm not going to mother you as to what exactly you need to buy. But certain items can be picked up pretty inexpensively at present.

For example, the popularity of trainers and deck shoes has created a massive over-supply of smart leather shoes, and dedicated shoe shops are feeling the pinch. You can pick up plenty of bargains here. Also, consider buying shoes that can be repaired. In this way you can extend the life of a favourite pair for a small extra cost.

For most people suits will be the most expensive essential items in their wardrobe. Unless you have a certain number of suits, you are going to wear them out pretty quickly. So perhaps it might prove cheaper to buy some suits second-hand. Charity shops, like Oxfam, have a steady supply at knockdown prices.

Charity shops also provide a rich source of material for fun, cheap and affordable fashion, well worth using for fancy dress parties and formal occasions, like weddings or balls, where smart dress is required. It might prove cheaper to get your own tails or other togs second-hand than spend a fortune hiring out such get-ups from the likes of Moss Bros.

Ah, such delicate decisions!

Telephone

Telecom charges change so rapidly at the moment. Competition is hotting up and various providers, new and old, are all bidding for your custom. In this climate, where there are so many deals to consider, it is impossible to give much specific guidance. Just remember to keep a few Foolish principles in mind.

Whether you use a land line or mobile connection, the main costs to consider are the standing charges and the rates for different varieties of call, either local, national or international. The standing charges are fixed costs for connection, which cannot change. The variable call charges, on the other hand, rise or fall depending on how often you use the phone and what type of call you are making.

Given this, you will have to work out how often you use the phone and why. If you use a telephone line for connection to the Internet, which costs the same as a local call, then you want the cheapest rate for local calls. If on the other hand you live in London and frequently ring your mother who lives in the Shetland Isles, you might want to find the telecom company that charges the least for national calls.

Be careful, though, of the swings and roundabouts when considering the best connection. For cheap local calls, you might be charged an exorbitant flat standing charge. Never judge one charge in isolation from another. A Web site worth looking at is **www.phonebills.org.uk**, which is sponsored by the telecom regulator Oftel. This compares telephone costs for consumers and helps you to wade through the various options.

Also, ask yourself if you really need a mobile as well as a land line. Work out how often you use one or the other. Does the one you use less frequently charge a higher standing charge? Then disconnect it immediately and cancel the account. This is a luxury. Do you find yourself taking calls on your mobile when you are near a land line? What a waste! Office lines are generally more efficient. If you need a mobile for business purposes, then ask your employers whether they can supply you with one.

With 24 million mobiles now in use in the UK, this last paragraph might seem churlish. The recent rise in mobile use has happened as a result of 'pay as you talk' pre-paid packages. Again be Foolish when looking at these deals. Work out how often you use the mobile phone. If you use it regularly it may not be the best deal, since the call charges for these pre-pay options can be much more expensive than if you take out a regular contract. If, on the other hand, you use the phone sparsely and keep it for emergencies only, then this pre-pay package could be the one for you.

Relax a little, lie back and luxuriate!

Take a deep breath, breathe out and relax. You have now looked at those parts of your financial picture you have to live with. Tidy them up and cut costs on these aspects, and you are well on your way to releasing money to target at investments. Elom, a writer on the *Living Below Your Means* board, followed this pattern and testifies: 'The best thing is that now I control my money rather than it controlling me.'

Having worked out how much you have to spend each month on essentials, you will now have an idea of what is left over. This surplus is yours to do with what you will. But before you run off thinking the world's your oyster, remember that not all luxuries are the same. Some are more luxurious than others. For example, a bottle of champagne to celebrate the end of the working week is probably going a bit over the top, whereas a Monday morning cappuccino to ease you back into the office after the weekend might prove less of a strain on your finances.

Again, you must subdivide your luxuries into essentials and less vital ones. Thus debt repayments, which are not necessarily something you have to do, but are definitely a useful way of getting you into a position to invest, should rank pretty high up the scale. Perhaps you reckon a holiday is a virtual necessity in your stressful position. That should come near the top as well.

Once you have ranked these things from your most essential luxury to your least important, you will have more of an idea of how vital it is that you choose to go racing above getting a new television. You can decide whether you are better off buying a new golf club or taking a date to the cinema. All these qualitative judgements can be made against a Foolish backdrop.

How you spend your extra non-essential money is up to you. There are literally a zillion money-saving tips to apply to each method of spending money. It would be silly to list them all here. Nevertheless I list some of my own favourites in the next section to show a typical Fool in action. The beauty of the Internet is that you can swap ideas with millions of others. The Motley Fool's *Living Below Your Means* board is a perfect example of this. So log on for further ideas. For the moment you're stuck with mine!

After deciding what luxuries you want to continue and which ones you want to curtail, you should arrive at a sum you can comfortably afford to put aside each month. Depending on your particular situation, this can go towards paying off your outstanding debts, or towards regular saving and investment plans, of which more in part two.

One Fool's cut-price luxuries

Being a keen golfer I used to buy golf magazines regularly, mainly to read when I was travelling on the train. I have given up lately though. These glossy monthlies purport to contain all the latest news and views from the golfing scene, as well as a wealth of informative features and helpful hints. All for £3.50. Despite this, almost half the 200-page publication is taken up by ads, and a lot of the rest is merely filling space with repetitive articles regurgitating the basic ideas of the handful of journalists working on it. I think it is the same for most monthly magazines that appeal to interest groups.

If you are a magazine fan, why not give up this extortionate practice and pick up some classic novels to read on the train instead? There has been a massive price war in this category lately. No copyright exists for authors after a certain period beyond their deaths, so book publishers can reprint their works cheaply. You can pick up some of the all-time great works of literature for under £2. Why skim through a mag which has taken a few weeks to put together when, for the same price or less, you can read a book into which the author has poured several years of his life?

On the subject of books, second-hand book shops also provide rich pickings for bargain hunters. I defy anyone not to find something worth reading here. Don't bother wasting your money on the latest new books, which may prove to be a waste of time and just a piece of publisher's puff.

In the so-called information age you shouldn't have to pay for any raw news. Most newspapers now publish their content for free on the Internet, as do other news providers, such as the BBC, Reuters and the Press Association. You have access to as many basic sources as a journalist via the Internet, and do not have to pay a premium to get up to speed with reporters. This means you can cut out the middleman and choose which interpretation of the news you want to read, rather than relying on someone else's version of events. You could probably find thousands of Web sites designed for those interested in golf, to take just one example!

The Internet is changing the way many transactions are done. Suppose you want to decorate your walls with some pictures. You could go to your local poster shop and spend a small fortune on random prints ripped out of old books, coloured and framed. Alternatively, look at some of the auctioneers online and you might be able to pick up watercolours, actually painted by some artist, for the same price. The market place is widening and prices are coming down as a result.

Music is rapidly falling in price online as well. All compact discs are becoming budget compact discs. At the same time, the choice is getting wider. Retailers like Amazon can put the whole music publishers' CD catalogue online, ready for ordering. Old-style record shops could only display a small proportion of such extensive catalogues. And the great thing about e-shopping is that you can browse without buying for as long as you wish. PC window-shopping is a perfect way to resist the urge to spend.

Other luxuries you can pick up cheaply include stand-by West End theatre tickets in the last two hours before the performance. Even if you don't get in, you can always nip off to the cinema instead.

You want to go on holiday? Why not consider renting a cottage with some friends rather than staying in expensive hotels? This is much cheaper and more fun. The Internet has become a bargain hunter's paradise in the travel department, too. Serious travellers might want to look at the Lonely Planet's comprehensive Web site (**www.lonelyplanet.com**) for tips and information from kindred spirits. A great place to look for cheap flights, holidays, and hotels on the spur of the moment is **www.lastminute.com**. As the name suggests, this British merchant has developed one of the UK's most original online ideas.

Finally, one sure way of boosting your financial picture is to give up smoking, if you are on the weed at the moment. These nicotine sticks have leapt in price, as they are an easy target for a Chancellor of the Exchequer, keen to boost the Government's revenue without raising income taxes. Duty on cigarettes this decade has outstripped inflation by immense amounts. As Raimesh, a Fool on the *Living Below Your Means* board states, 'Smoking … is one of the worst ways of losing money. Twenty a day costs you over £100 per month in cigarettes. That adds up to £1,200 a year.'

This chapter has looked at only one side of Mr Micawber's cash equation: outgoings. We have assumed your income is constant. If you find that after paring down your essentials to a minimum and curbing your luxuries as much as possible, you still have no spare cash to clear your debts and start investing with, then we need to look at your income. Obviously this isn't large enough to cater for the way you want to lead your life. It's time to consider how you earn your cash.

Emergency funds vs. insurance
Before moving on to look at where to invest the cash you have gleaned, it is worth considering the tricky issue of what funds you should keep in reserve for emergencies. The beast we call life sometimes rears up and kicks us in the face. Your boss might suddenly decide to lay off your whole

department. You have to give up work in any case, until your hip heals from the high jinks you got up to in the Alps last Christmas. All manner of tragedies like this or worse can befall you at any stage. You never know what life might bring.

Given this, should you prepare for such eventualities, or just let the fates decide the outcome? Whilst there's no point worrying too much about what has yet to happen, it may be worth giving yourself a buffer against the unforeseen. Before you start to invest, perhaps you should get together an emergency cash fund of a few thousand pounds or so to pay for the things you simply must have.

Beyond that, be wary of any general insurance schemes against accidents, illnesses and redundancy. These premiums can mount up outrageously and then be most ungenerous when the accident happens, the money bound in by murky terms and conditions.

Obviously you must make a decision based on your own particular position. If you are the main breadwinner in the household and have to support several members of your family, then it is most important for you to check what protection you are guaranteed by your employer, mortgage company and others if you can no longer work, for example, or if you die early.

If you don't have people to support then the decision is probably easier. In any case it's worth setting aside a little cash for emergencies before you begin to invest, since investing is a long-term process and you should only use cash you won't need for the next five years at least.

Ten Foolish ways to glean cash

We all have more cash than we think. Saving money can be less lonely if done together. Look at the Motley Fool's *Living Below your Means* message board for inspiration.

1. Divide the things on which you spend money each month into essentials and luxuries.

2. Pay for essential items first. Then you can sit back and enjoy the unexpected pleasures of life, without worrying about the bills.

3. Try to cut the costs of essential items as much as possible.

4. Pay unavoidable bills which you can't make any cheaper, like council tax and water rates, by direct debit and forget about them.

5. Negotiate down the charges on your gas and electricity bills. Consider getting both provided by the same supplier at a cheaper rate.

6. Avoid running a car if you possibly can.

7. Don't eat out too much. Make your own lunch once a week. Learn to cook.

8. Buy your clothes for the year when the sales are on.

9. Work out how often you use a mobile telephone. Go to www.phonebills.org to see if you can get a better deal on your home telephone connection.

10. Relax a little, lie back and luxuriate. Pick out your most essential luxuries and savour them.

Chapter Three – Pay in your pocket

Money is like muck, not good except if it be spread.
Francis Bacon, *Essays, Of Seditions and Troubles*

From the last two chapters you will have learnt that cash is a vital commodity if you want to get into a position to invest. But of course you didn't need me to tell you that. We all know that cash is the oil that helps the globe to turn smoothly. Without the folding stuff we wouldn't be able to do much.

Now, think back to the first time you worked for money. Can you recall the thrill of receiving payment for your services? You can't? I know it's hard to recreate that feeling. As you become more used to earning, you accept that working is, for most people, a normal state of affairs. But it's time for a little history lesson.

At school I was taught about the famous missionary and explorer of Africa, David Livingstone. Long before setting out on his travels, he spent his first working week in a mill near Glasgow. At the end of his labours, the virtuous thirteen-year-old rushed home and gave half his earnings to his mother. The rest he spent on self-improving books. (Unfortunately the Fool wasn't available. It hadn't been invented back in the 1820s. And young David couldn't get on the Net. At that time the World Wide Web had more to do with spiders or the international spinning trade than the electronic distribution of information.)

You may think Livingstone was just a goody-two-shoes, but his lesson shows how he valued his earning capability. It was vitally important for his later life. The books he bought and read and learnt from became the bricks and mortar on which he built his famous career. But hang on, why do we want to know about the early life of a Victorian icon?

Well, living conditions today are becoming more and more like those in Livingstone's day. OK, teenagers aren't being shoved down coal mines and the 72-hour week, spread over six days, is no longer the average. But, as in Livingstone's time, a job for life is no longer the norm for most earners. Instead, work is more precarious and unpredictable than it has been at any time since the 1930s.

However, the job for life shouldn't necessarily be mourned. Toilers should rejoice that the chains of such an existence have been broken. You can now exploit your unique skills and talents as never before. From now on it will not be uncommon for a school-leaver to have as many as ten different jobs during his working lifetime. Such a varied career should be welcomed rather than worried about.

In a Foolish way, this means that you, as an individual, have the power to decide what jobs you want to do and how you want to earn money, rather than relying on an old-style paternalistic local employer for a living. No more will you have to doff your Foolish cap to your boss. Instead, consider that you are helping him through your endeavours, rather than the other way round. No longer do you have to feel forever in his debt and thank him for helping you with his kind provision of employment. You are working together in a joint enterprise.

But at the same time, no longer can you rely on one organization to pay you for forty years, and then, providing you don't make much fuss, reward you with a carriage clock and keep you safe and solvent in retirement on a company pension. Wave goodbye to this boring tram-lined existence. Kick off those comfortable retirement slippers. And say hello to the more variable lifestyle of the here and now. Embrace the future! You have the control to do the tasks to which you are most suited, rather than those your employer finds to keep you busy. It's up to you to decide what you want to do for a living.

If this prospect scares rather than inspires you, then take comfort in the fact that although large employers are shedding jobs left, right and centre, at the same time the labour market is far more flexible. More jobs are being created in new growing sectors of the fast-moving economy. Take my own foolish existence in the world of publishing. Twenty years ago, few journalists could write a word in anger for a newspaper or magazine without being a member of the National Union of Journalists. Editors were stuck with the opinions of old hacks, and so were readers. Similarly, Equity, the actors' union, still tends to strangle the prospects of new talent struggling to make the grade, rather than encouraging it.

This stultifying situation worked fine for some, but if this static system had remained in place the exciting changes of the media world, which now allows people to write for a wider variety of publications, could never have happened. Only two years ago, few established writers would have dreamt of leaving a secure job on a leading newspaper for the horizons of the World Wide Web. Today, more and more are leaving the closed shop for the open arena of the Internet. Soon there will be more writers employed online than there will be writing copy for the old media.

So in such an era of fast-paced change, it may not be beneficial to be tied to one office stool. The whole office block may be computerized and pulverized into one room, manned by a handful of loyal retainers (or more likely sharp-suited professionals), before you have earned even one of the hours on your carriage clock retirement gift!

Imagine, for instance, you had chosen to work in the same textile mill as David Livingstone, but in the early 1970s – or, at the same time, at the London docks or perhaps down a Welsh coal mine. By now, in the late 1990s, only a handful of the colleagues you started your working life with would still be employed. Few would be able to find work in these fields, such is the decay of these traditional industries in modern service-led Britain.

If instead you had learnt how to program the computers that now perform many modern mechanized roles, your venture, although perhaps initially perceived as risky, would have paid off handsomely and you would have a whole clutch of colleagues by now. Such nimbleness and appropriately fleet-footed decision-making are necessary for survival and success in today's modern economy, which requires a work force with specialized skills.

But this flexibility also means that, if you know where to work, the cash gleaning process can become much easier. Rather than sweating to save some shrapnel, you can raise your income by tailoring your working life to your own needs, rather than those of your white-collared factory proprietor with the pension he periodically dangles under your nose!

Boost your income Foolishly!

In the last chapter we looked at ways of gleaning cash by constricting your money outflow and conserving your income through penny-pinching. But of course, the alternative to reducing your outgoings is boosting your incomings. So far we haven't discussed this other side of the coin. This cash boosting exercise could prove much more Foolish than some saving scheme that requires massive amounts of willpower.

Most money-savers, when calculating what they want to save, reckon that their earnings remain pretty constant. But if you can bolster them, this will lift your cash balances no end, or quickly belittle your debt. The extra time required to improve your income will also eat into the spare time during which you probably fritter your cash away on frivolous entertainment. If you are working, you will have less time to spend your earnings, and consequently your money situation will pick up immeasurably through this double whammy of work.

Now consider your present income. Presumably it comes from a normal nine-to-five style bread-winning exercise. If you enjoy the job, you might ask your boss about the possibility of doing overtime. But if you can't bear to spend a single moment more in the office, look beyond the confines of those four walls. You might want to work in a pub for instance. That way, as one frugal Fool put it, you can have a laugh and a chat if the boozer isn't too busy. Also, punters might buy you drinks if you're lucky.

What if you don't fancy pulling pints, or serving meals? Take stock of your hobbies instead. Think about what you like doing outside work. If you like sport, you could go and offer to help out coaching sports teams. Do you play a musical instrument? If so, you could audition for a local orchestra, or maybe teach your instrument. Even better, form a band and play for money in the same pub you didn't fancy pulling pints in. Perhaps you like going to nightclubs and dancing? Why not help out the promoter, by depositing flyers around town? Or alternatively offer your skills as a dancer! You could sing in a choir or a band if you like belting out tunes in the bath. Perhaps you have a historical turn of mind. In that case, volunteer to go on an archaeological dig at weekends. If you collect something, you might try and run a market stall. Or, even better in these wired times, you could easily set up your own e-business. An easy way to see if this could work is to check out the Web sites of online auctioneers, E-Bay (**www.ebay.co.uk**), Qxl (**www.qxl.com**), or iCollector (**www.icollector.com**). Here, you can find out how well you know the prices for the particular goods you intend to start selling or dealing in.

Admittedly, most of these secondary occupations won't reap huge amounts of cash. But that's not necessarily the point. If you're desperately trying to save to invest, most of these jobs won't cost you anything except time, which previously you may have used to spend your precious principal income in.

Finally you could learn a party trick, practise it to perfection then go down the pub and ask your friends how much they will give you if, for instance, you balance a full pint of beer on top of your head for a minute, without spilling a drop. By this method you could enjoy a night's entertainment pretty cheaply. If you are any good you might be able to make some money out of it, too.

First, the main source of bounty

However, before putting your tantalizing plans for boosting your earnings into action, you should sort out your main source of income. Far be it for others to tell you what exactly you should do for a living. No, that would be a most Wise thing to do. Here, though, you will find an offering of Foolish principles which you may find useful in your hunt for a job, and some other hints to bear in mind when trying to secure a position.

In 1086, William the Conqueror (of 1066 fame) commissioned the Domesday book as a survey of the land of the Angles (Angleland), which he had recently won. He wanted, very Foolishly, to find out what his new-found wealth was worth, and what he could expect in terms of services from his loyal Norman subjects and not-so-loyal Anglo-Saxon ones. In other words, he conducted the biggest audit ever done up to that point.

Many crusty historians think these two weighty Domesday tomes the most convincing example of the feudal system in action. What on earth is the feudal system, you might Foolishly ask? Well, in those days money wasn't so important to poor Fools working in the fields. Many were indeed serfs, known also as villeins. Rather than being paid for their services, they were tied 'feudally' to their lords. In return for this cheap labour, the lord offered them protection. Villeins could also have a few days off each week to work on their own crops. And just as the serfs worked for the local lord, the lord owed feudal dues to his sovereign the King in return for holding the land. This was paid in military service, used to protect the sovereignty of the whole realm in times of danger.

Thus everyone in the system had a role to play to ensure that society prospered and was free from attack. Now this feudal ideal was fine in theory, but open to much abuse. It only took a few people to break the rules and the whole practice started to come apart at the seams. Lords could skive off military service by paying taxes. After the Black Death came along, wiping out a third of the working population, serfs started to clamour for payment for their increasingly valuable services. And the first major down-tools in English history took place in 1381 with the Peasants' Revolt. Then, in the following century, lords had their chance to put right their differences with the monarchy in the Wars of the Roses, which saw rebel groups of courtiers fight for control of the crown. This civil war put an end to the old system of military organization through feudal service.

From now on, if someone wanted something he had to pay for it. The post-war ideal of a job for life has also turned out to be as fragile as the feudal system. Change the economic rules a little and full employment goes out of the window, with all its attendant benefits of security and assured pensions for former employees. Rather than continually ploughing the same furrow, yesterday's office peasants can now decide where to plant themselves. By sowing skill seeds throughout your working life, you can continue to reap rich harvests throughout your cropping career. Stick with the same outmoded skill and you might find the soil becomes tired and unable to support that style of working anymore.

Consider your career as a series of services that you are providing for your various employment lords, so that the fertile business sector you are ploughing together will provide plenty of bounty for both lords and the lorded (that's you). Try to value your service along these lines. If you have something strong to offer, then treat your employment contract as a negotiating tool.

Take a lesson from professional footballers. These highly talented individuals used to be regarded as loyal servants of a particular club. The general public, and the majority of professional footballers themselves, tended to think how lucky they were to be able to play football for a living. The chairmen of football league clubs prospered from this amateur attitude, keeping expenses to a minimum. This meant the majority of gate revenue was distributed in dividends amongst the owners of the club.

Up until the 1960s, the football clubs had agreed amongst themselves a *maximum* wage they would pay players. This capping measure was designed to stop expensive transfers and wage inflation. It also deterred efforts to buy in talent. The clubs feared that, if allowed to run free, this ugly process would in turn lead to spiralling expenses and dwindling profits. Oh how David Beckham and the Manchester United squad would laugh if the club chairman Martin Edwards tried to impose this limit nowadays!

But today's stars have to thank the players of the 1960s, led by future BBC television commentator Jimmy Hill, for breaking the owners' stranglehold and so opening up the path to the current well-paid status they enjoy. In a sense football has left its feudal roots behind, and assumed a modern compensation system based on services rendered.

Special agents now represent footballers to argue their case. They reckon that without top footballers, no crowds would turn up. And without strong popular support, nobody would buy associated club merchandise, and television companies wouldn't pay to televise matches. So footballers are central to this process of bringing in revenue. Hence their agents try to make sure their clients take a certain proportion of these proceeds. As television companies squabble for the right to broadcast games and subsequently pay ever-higher fees, so stars like Beckham see their salaries escalate. Beckham himself has become a business. He is the lord of the playing field rather than the servant of the football club.

Now I am not suggesting that you storm up to your boss on Monday, drop your keyboard on his desk and refuse to work until he gives you more of the company's turnover as just compensation for your tireless endeavours! Remember everybody's situation is different. You might not be the David Beckham of your sales team. And you wouldn't be particularly pleased if your boss turned to you and told you to take a fifty per cent salary cut, because someone in marketing had made a boo-boo that had halved sales that year.

Before starting a job, though, do assess the benefits you are being offered in the employment package as a whole, not just the headline salary. Before the 1980s, when employers offered feudal security, your salary and pension were the only things that mattered. Now that employees are more of a disposable commodity, it is also conversely true that the workers who help the company to grow and prosper should be highly valued, like David Beckham.

Look, in particular, at what your overall package offers in terms of a share in the fortunes of the enterprise. Such incentives might be profit share schemes, stock options, employee share ownership plans and simple bonus rewards. All of these are becoming increasingly important, and decent employers should be happy to offer them. Such incentive schemes make staff more keenly interested in enhancing the company's performance, since they benefit from it as well.

If instead you are fobbed off with other marginal perks, like health insurance or season ticket loans, be very careful. Explore all avenues before accepting such alternatives. Remember both these types of benefit are more feudal than modern. Admittedly most employers would prefer you to be fit and healthy for work, and want you to come in to the office on time rather than wait for an off-peak cheap day return every morning. But these simple things cost less than you might imagine, and are less valuable than incentive schemes that spread profits out to employees. A large firm can negotiate a cheap collective deal for employee health insurance, and probably insure itself against some of its employees falling ill and affecting the business as a whole in the process. If such peripheral perks might, you feel, affect your total compensation agreement, then perhaps inquire whether you can forego them in return for other more material monetary benefits, such as the schemes outlined above.

Incentive scheme details

It is useful to understand the main details offered by various employee incentive schemes, so that you know where you stand before negotiating with your employer. Remember, though, that you will probably find it hard to demand one scheme or another. Your employer will want to make the process as simple as possible, and will be unwilling to offer different schemes to individual employees. You may have to talk with your colleagues to come to some agreement.

The bonus is probably the oldest and most traditional incentive. This is usually paid once a year, either around Christmas or at the end of the tax year. This is perhaps the simplest idea to understand. Effectively it is an extra cash payment, decided upon by the employer according to how he thinks you have performed over the previous year. The problem is that this can be arbitrary, based purely on the employer's opinion.

A slightly more open scheme is the profit share plan. It is very popular, particularly amongst sales staff. As the name suggests, it entitles you to a share of any company profits. Normally this would be net profits rather than gross profits, calculated after normal operating expenses but before the impact of additional expenses. Again, work out particular percentages before deciding on this scheme.

Employee share ownership schemes, or ESOPs, are also becoming increasingly popular. These allow employees to own a little bit of their company by buying shares at preferential prices. If you are committed to the company you work for and envisage working there for some time, this can be a very good scheme to adopt. You will share in the fortunes of the company, whether they are good or bad. And if the company decides to float and make its shares more widely available, then you can sell them openly and reap handsome rewards. You can get tax breaks on these schemes as well.

Share option schemes are similar to ESOPs in that they allow employees to share directly in the fortunes of the company. They give the holder the right to purchase company shares at a particular price, and normally for a certain amount of time. Obviously if the company's shares are listed on the Stock Exchange, making them easily tradable, then share option schemes are more immediately useful. Some company schemes are tax-efficient as well. These can be the most Foolish and generous options of all incentive schemes.

When negotiating such delicate matters of compensation you may not be able to afford an agent, like David Beckham, but bear in mind that if a headhunter or recruitment consultant introduced you to the prospective employer, then he or she is on your side. Recruitment specialists benefit from whatever extra salary or other packages you negotiate, so treat them as you would an agent to fight your corner.

Once you are in employment, you should be wary about such tough negotiation. Concentrate on the job in hand and let your tasks speak for themselves. If you wish to say anything, it's best to bring it up during your scheduled reviews, normally held annually. Few employers like pushy employees who are more intent on their own remuneration than the company's wellbeing. This can actually harm the company, particularly if dissent spreads. Only air your views about your pay when invited to. The ideal is, as mentioned above, to find a compensation scheme that benefits you as the company's performance improves. This should prove sufficient incentive for you to do the job to the best of your ability.

Incentive schemes like these should also show you whether you are in the right job. If, after a while in a particular position, you still find work a struggle, the company fails to perform better, and you and your colleagues have had hardly any benefit from your incentive scheme, then something's quite obviously wrong. Either your company is not growing, and could go out of business in the longer run (in which case, prepare to go and find another position); or else you are not working efficiently, because you fail to derive any benefit or reward from your hard work. Perhaps, more hopefully, you will reap dividends over a longer period of time. Whatever the scenario, you must keep Foolishly assessing your position at work: such is the modern way!

Having sorted out your income Foolishly, you are now ready to start using the surplus to either clear your debts or even start investing. But before you get too excited and eagerly turn the page, there is one expensive outlay I said I'd cover back in the frugal chapter on saving: property, mortgages and the great renting-versus-buying debate. So take a deep breath – this cash-eating monster has to be tackled.

By the way, are you thinking there is one big item I haven't accounted for yet? That managed pension plan you contribute a certain amount to each month? If you are in debt, this could prove more disastrous to your long term financial plans than many other investment techniques. WHAT! you shout. These Fools have completely lost their marbles now if they think they can take this plank away from me. But hold on while we sort out the roof over your head, which could be leaking away as much cash as the charges on your pension plan. We shall return to this topic in Chapter Five.

Working whilst studying
Ask most students why they are at university and they will say, to

have fun and enjoy themselves during their youth with friends of their own age. More conscientious undergraduates might claim they are there to study their subject. An increasing proportion of careerist students might think they are studying in order to get a better job than they would without the vital piece of paper they are trying to obtain. Few students would say they are at university to work. By work, I mean earn money rather than study books and attend lectures.

Well, in an ideal world that should be true. But as we know, being a student is more expensive than ever before. First decide what you want to get out of university. You will be working in a job for forty years after graduation, so working when at university might seem a waste of those precious years. If you agree, consider other ways of saving money, as outlined in earlier chapters, before you start toiling for cash. By living with your parents, you could save a lot of money on expensive accommodation away from home. But this might restrict the freedom from the parental bosom you are expecting to enjoy at university.

Another solution might be to work just during your holidays, so that you are free to enjoy university japes and jollities to the full during term-time. If, on the other hand, you plan to use the long vacations to travel and explore far-flung corners of the world, while you still don't have any restrictions such as a job with twenty days' holiday a year, this plan might not suit your needs so well. Maybe, then, you should find some part-time work whilst at university. Working for university organizations may prove more advantageous than for external employers, since they will be more sympathetic to your predicament of balancing study, work and play. Work during the term as long as it doesn't affect what you want to get out of university. After all you'll get plenty of work experience afterwards!

Basic employment rights

Employers are legally obliged to provide certain things, whether written in a contract or not, when they offer you a full-time job. These include:

A minimum wage of £3.60 per hour (as of 1 February 2000).

A pay chit detailing exact remuneration and deductions, such as tax and national insurance.

One week's notice of dismissal, after you have worked for one month in the job.

Four weeks' annual paid holiday, after working for thirteen weeks in the job.

Certain statutory payment for medically enforced absence.

Fourteen weeks' maternity leave, rising to forty weeks after you have been employed for one year.

Employment legislation is extremely complicated. The list given above is intended only as a guide, summarizing the most basic points to consider. For more up-to-date information, take a look at the Department of Trade & Industry's Web site – **www.dti.gov.uk/IR/index.htm**. *If you click on this page you will see how complex the whole issue is. If you have any problems at work, send your employer there. He may be even more alarmed!*

Ten Foolish ways to perk up your pay

1. **The job for life is over but shouldn't necessarily be mourned.** Rather than relying on an old-style cradle-to-grave employer, you have the freedom to choose exactly how to earn your income.
2. **The labour market is now far more flexible than ever before** with many jobs being created by the faster-growing sectors of the economy.
3. **The alternative to reducing your outgoings by painful penny-pinching is to boost your income.** If you can't bear the thought of overtime in your main job, perhaps take a

part-time job in a pub.

4. Consider making your hobby an alternative source of income. Even if it doesn't work out you will have still enjoyed yourself and may have stopped yourself from spending money in that time.

5. Think of yourself as David Beckham and your main employer as Manchester United. You are providing them with a skill and should negotiate for adequate compensation.

6. Any negotiation is best done when starting a job. If you have a recruitment consultant working for you, regard the person as your agent.

7. Consider the whole benefits package you are offered. The 'extras' are easy for an employer to provide and should be regarded as part of your 'compensation'. See if you can take them as salary instead.

8. Work out the details of any incentive scheme you are offered carefully.

9. Once in employment be wary of tough negotiation. No one wants to work with a troublesome employee. Only talk about such matters at your annual review meeting.

10. Keep assessing your position at work. Should you stay or should you go?

Chapter Four – A roof over your head?

'Mid pleasures and palaces though we may roam,
Be it ever so humble, there's no place like home.
John Howard Payne (1791–1852)

At the end of each day, whoever we are and whatever we do, we all have to find somewhere to sleep, a place to rest our weary limbs in readiness for the next day's challenges and assaults. Hopefully, this hunt isn't a nightly preoccupation for you – though the Fool has nothing against promiscuous nocturnal activity, as long as it doesn't take one's mind off the investment game in the long run.

Most of us require a place we can call home. You might still have the travelling bug, a deep desire to explore parts of the globe still barely mapped out, discover sights few tourists have seen and experience hedonistic pleasures even fewer have enjoyed. But at the end of your sojourn, you are still going to have to find four walls within which to store the assorted paraphernalia you have collected to remind you of your trips.

And if you want to work or borrow money to pay for your travels, your employer and bank are going to demand an address where they can reach or catch you. This insurance measure means your boss can march around to wake you up if you're late into the office. More worryingly, the bank can, if you default on loans, also send the bailiffs around to collect payment in kind if they have to. This might mean the sad and early break-up of your precious collection of odds and ends picked up on foreign shores. Wave goodbye to that tribal mask you picked up for £2.50 in the New Hebrides.

The drawback of living on a crowded island such as Britain is that there just isn't really enough space for everyone. After a long day of trekking through the Papuan Highlands, you may have been able to pitch your tent on the nearest patch of flat grass in the forest, hostile tribes notwithstanding. But if you try to do the same thing on Peckham Rise, you will be politely asked to move along by a member of the local constabulary.

You could possibly move back in with your own particular tribe. Initially, your parents may welcome you back warmly to the family fold, relieved that you have survived your holiday abroad. However, after a time you might find that you have outgrown the nest. Following your fully fledged flight into the big wide world, you may discover the warm parental bosom constricts your ability to spread your wings. Once your parents have resumed their old habit of sending you to your room for being late for supper, you may think it's time to move on and re-assert your independence elsewhere. In any case your folks may be getting a bit fed up as well, thinking that they at least deserve some housekeeping money for all their efforts.

Moving out

What are your options now then? Well if you want a place of your own, you have a basic decision to make between renting a spot off someone else, whether with friends, relatives or your lover, or else actually taking the plunge and buying a property of your own. Yikes! This second decision requires some serious Foolish financial consideration, because as I mentioned above, this island is small and crowded, property is in short supply and there is hot demand in certain favoured areas.

Whether you rent or buy, much, in fact virtually everything, depends on your own particular cash position and prospects. Unless you are pretty flush, in which case you're probably not finding this book that relevant to your needs, buying a property will normally involve borrowing a significant sum of money. These home loans are called mortgages. And mortgages are like marriages. They should not be undertaken lightly, since once you are hitched with one it will take a lot of effort to untie yourself. So the contract you choose should be considered a long-term obligation.

OK, this is all getting too deadly serious. Let's leave the big M until a little later and lighten up for a while. The one thing to remember when thinking about where to buy is to find somewhere you would be happy to stay, even if your situation changed and circumstances meant you couldn't afford to move. If you accept that we all have to stay somewhere, then you might as well like the spot you intend to spend most of your sleeping, and a lot of your waking, hours.

Buying a home takes a frustratingly irregular amount of time because of the nature of the housing market, which is made up of many different types of people, each with different requirements and resources. Don't get drawn too easily into this game of snakes and ladders. Always assess the inherent worth of your prospective property as a home and decide whether it meets your needs. Then and only then, after weighing up your available funding options, consider making an offer. In this way, even if you are not a financial winner in the property game, you should still be happy about where you live, since that was your first consideration rather than the financial aspect of the transaction.

Remember that a roof over your head is an essential part of living, and not a means of making money. Finding accommodation shouldn't be confused with long-term investing. Most people have to go into debt, via a mortgage, to 'invest' in property. And we found out how detrimental debt can be to long-term investing in Chapter One.

For this reason, buying a property shouldn't be perceived as a short-term gamble, as it quite often is, sometimes by quite rational people who have been egged on by avaricious estate agents to look at prices before property. It can be a risky game to play unless done for the long term. You have to live somewhere, but you can invest elsewhere and not solely in your accommodation.

That said, there are significant differences between stepping on to the property ladder and staying on the free and easy open ground of renting. Both cost significant sums of money. You will have to decide which is more economical for your particular situation. Let's look at each in turn.

Rent a room and the world's your oyster

There can't be many people who haven't rented a sleeping spot at some time during their lives. It doesn't have to have been your own home. For instance you may have spent a night in a four star hotel in central Paris. Perhaps you have stopped off at a motel in the Midwest of America. Or you could have holed up in a B&B in a seedy seaside resort on the South Coast. But in all these situations you will have rented a space off the proprietor for the evening. Admittedly this is a very, very short-term lease arrangement, organized to cover your immediate needs. All you need is to have enough cash to pay for the room. But the principle behind the transaction remains the same, whatever lodging you want to rent and for whatever length of time.

This shows how flexible renting can be, allowing you to put your head down wherever you wish, with few ties or obligations. What wonderful freedom to roam! However, after a while you might get tired of living out of a suitcase and want to settle down in a slightly more permanent spot. In any case, sleeping in a different place each night and hiring rooms by the daily rate could get quite pricey, even if you stayed at the cheapest dive in the district you eventually want to live in.

Renting a place is only a touch more tricky than finding a hotel room. Just as the owner of a hotel requires some identification, or an address so he can chase you if you don't pay up, so there are certain things you will probably have to settle with the landlord before you move into his property.

He, or she, may well require references, either from your employer or some previous landlord. If you haven't rented before, then a friend who can vouch for your honesty and trustworthiness should suffice. More importantly, you will have to put down a deposit, which is normally equivalent to a month's rent. Satisfy these two requirements and you can take up residence straight away. Similarly you can check out, as with a hotel room, as long as you give reasonable notice of your plan to do so. If instead you had a mortgage on a house it would be harder to extract yourself at short notice.

There must be more to it than that, you cry. Well, I suppose the most important thing, before we come on to the monetary aspect, is the agreement you will have to sign with your landlord about the terms of your lease. The simplest and most popular form nowadays is the assured short-term leasehold agreement. This normally lasts for a minimum of six months. Check this carefully before you sign it.

The contract should cover most things. First of all, it should lay out the basic terms such as the exact length of the lease and precise cost of renting the property. Other important points should also be covered, including what rights of access the landlord has to the place, and what notice period is required on either side before termination or renewal of the rental agreement. Check other terms such as those about the furnishings – make up and sign an inventory of all the items in the flat that belong to the landlord before moving in, so there is no confusion over goods. Also confirm other ground rules such as whether you can keep pets or smoke on the property.

Leases can of course last for longer periods of time. The agreements covering these can become progressively more complicated the longer the rental term. During a six-month short-hold tenancy you will be more concerned about the specific terms for use of the property. But over a longer period you will start to become more interested in the length of the lease and your rights regarding the termination or renewal of the agreement. You may find many different clauses covering various scenarios, which could all affect what you pay.

The nitty-gritty

This brings us on to costs. How much should you expect to pay for a lease? Well, obviously this depends on the place you live in, what accommodation it offers and where it's located. All of these factors will affect the price. One way to discover the mean price for a particular lease is to find out the freehold value of the property. That is the amount it would cost you to purchase outright.

This may be a slightly hit and miss process if you compare prices for similar properties as advertised by estate agents. However, you can now find recent prices for different types of property throughout the UK at a useful Web site called **www.upyourstreet.com**. This will give an indication of how much it would cost to buy your intended property, though it is not entirely accurate, being only a very rough snapshot of the whole post-code district. Alternatively, contact the local council who rate each property in their area, putting them in different valuation bands in order to calculate the Council Tax.

Having found out this freehold price, you must now find the total rent collected from the property annually by the landlord. This is known as the annual rental yield. What? That sounds very Wise indeed, you might think. Well it is. We are putting ourselves into the landlord's position to discover how much he intends to make from renting out the property over a year.

Imagine finding out that the one-bedroom flat in South London you have your eyes on is valued at £100,000 by Lambeth Council, which sets the local Council Tax. Say the flat will cost you £500 to rent per month. Thus if you were to live in the property over a whole year you would have to fork out a scary £6,000. Divide the annual rental return by the freehold value and times it by a hundred, and you have the gross annual rental yield on the property, which works out at 6 per cent. After a year you will have paid for 6 per cent of the property or, more accurately, the landlord has already recouped 6 per cent of his outlay!

Of course, this assumes that he didn't have to borrow money to pay for the flat in the first place. Mortgage providers, who lend such capital sums, do tend to charge an interest rate above the rate of inflation on the loans they make. Also the net yield will be lower once maintenance and upkeep costs, which retain the value of the property, are added into the equation. These costs, at say £1,000 a year for a generous landlord, will knock the net rent down to £5,000 and hence the net rental yield down to 5 per cent. One of the advantages of renting is you don't have to spend money on keeping the property spick and span. You also don't have to worry about whether it is losing value.

In this way, you can compare various properties by their rental yields. The higher the yield the more expensive the property is to rent, relatively. Sometimes yields and hence rents can be bumped up to an extortionate rate because estate agents are employed to find tenants and manage the property, by for instance collecting rents and making repairs. This adds to the costs. Make sure as a tenant that these aren't passed on to your rental charges – in many cases they will be.

Now imagine taking out a longer lease on the same flat, say ten years at the same rate of £500 a month. This would cost £60,000 in all (£500 times 120 months). You would be mad to accept this, though, especially as you have to give the property back at the end of the lease. For that sum of money you might be able to buy a property yourself, if you wanted to. However, in this situation you can begin to appreciate how property investors put prices on houses – from their future revenue potential.

Revenue potential? Another Wise concept you might worry, what happened to all that fluffy Foolery we were fond of? Well when more people rented homes rather than owned them, the landlords valued their assets on the basis of how much revenue they would make from them. If you want to buy a place rather than rent one, you could consider this as well. Unfortunately you will not be able to buy a property outright, unless you are lucky. Instead you will have to borrow the money from a lender in the form of a mortgage. This complicates matters, since you have to factor in the monthly mortgage repayments before working out the return you would make from renting out your property. Say you bought the £100,000 Lambeth flat with a £95,000 mortgage, which you are repaying at the rate of £400 a month. This means you would only make £100 a month gross, before other costs, or £1,200 per year, a paltry net rental yield of 1.2 per cent.

In any case you have to live somewhere. Everyone needs a roof over their head. That's the basic premise of accommodation, whether you rent or buy your own place. If you are determined to stay where you are for a significant period of time because of work or family reasons, then you may not need the flexibility offered by renting. In any case, some wealth-seekers consider putting money into a landlord's grubby hands each month a particularly silly thing to do.

As we mentioned above, if you pay rent at the rate of £500 a month, which is not uncommon for central London, you will have waved goodbye to £6,000 by the end of the year. Put this sum towards paying for a property of your own and, although over half of it may go to the mortgage company in interest payments, at least you might end up retaining some capital in the form of bricks and mortar after twenty-five years of blood, toil and sweat.

If this home ownership dream inspires you, read on.

The property ladder!

Ah yes, the property ladder! Climbing on to it seems to be the eternal dream and prime occupation of many British people. It's almost a national obsession. Newspaper headlines are written incessantly about the subject. Property prices splurge forth from reporters' pens on a regular basis. Estate agents, who cream off tasty fees, are openly reviled. And once you have clambered on, mortgage rates rule homeowners' lives for the rest of their working days.

In short, it is the biggest investment most people ever make. Nothing else will put you in debt quite as much as buying a house. Most people who are investing whilst in this situation are effectively investing when they don't have any money. Homeowners borrow massive amounts of money on the back of the security of the property they intend to purchase. Then once they've just about settled down, it's time to try and move another rung up the ladder. Phew! What a sweat. It's made me tired just thinking about it all.

So before you take the plunge and join the treadmill, lading yourself with long-term debt in the process, consider the full implications of your move. Put it in the context of your present cash position. If you haven't got any money but want to invest, by buying property you unbalance the whole of your precarious portfolio ambitions. First of all, it is most unlikely that you will be able to buy a property straight away. You will need a deposit in order to get a mortgage, commonly as much as 5 per cent of the purchase price. It will take time to save up for that, particularly if you are already in debt.

Some mortgage providers do offer 100 per cent mortgages, allowing you to buy a property using borrowed money alone. But the other aspects of buying a property, such as lawyers, estate agency and surveying fees also cost a lot of money. Basically the whole process is very expensive and may put your investing plans out of kilter.

However, if you are renting you will still have to get a deposit together, usually. This won't be as punitive, but will probably be the equivalent of the first month's rent, as suggested above. You are going to have to get this cash together from somewhere. For cash-gleaning ideas, go back to the first two chapters.

A man's house may be his castle but, as we know, castles can be very expensive places to purchase outright. Instead let's aim our sights a little lower. Imagine your castle is the same flat we talked about renting in South London, with a freehold value of £100,000. Putting ourselves in the place of the landlord, we valued the property in terms of its future revenue potential. If rented out, the flat would bring in £5,000 a year after costs. This means it would take twenty years for the landlord to recoup the value of his initial outlay. But if you wanted to live in this flat and buy it outright from the landlord, how would you go about it?

Well let's say a building society has taken pity on you, or rather seen another mug coming, and decided to lend you the £100,000 as long as you pay it back within twenty-five years. This sum will pay for the flat outright. Remember you will still have to find all the additional expenses involved, such as solicitor's and surveyor's fees. Most mortgage providers will only lend people three times their annual salary. So in this instance you will need to be earning £33,333 a year at least. But getting hold of the initial sum is the easiest part of the whole process. Now you have the prospect of not only paying back the £100,000 capital sum, but also the interest on it.

You might gawk if I tell you that repaying the £100,000 sum will not be as tricky as paying off the interest. But it's true. Remember interest rates can fluctuate viciously. From 1945 to 1996, the average mortgage rate was 8.65 per cent, according to the *Compendium of Housing Finance Statistics 1997*. Let's take this figure and imagine that this will be the mean rate for the next twenty-five-years as well, when you will be paying back your mortgage. This means that you will pay an average of £699 each month, assuming you pay off none of your loan at all.

By the end of the twenty-five-year period, a little older and greyer and possibly more Foolish, you sign and send off your final cheque to the building society. The total amount you will have paid in interest for Home Sweet Home is a staggering £216,250! This would hardly surprise anyone who was sitting up and paying attention when we talked about compound interest in Chapter One. Even more frightening is that you still have to pay off the £100,000 capital sum originally loaned to you to pay for the house!

Starter mortgages, fixed vs. variable rates

If you're intent on buying property, there are hundreds of different mortgages you can choose from to satisfy this very English desire. There are places on the Web that are well worth visiting to look at comparative rates. You could look, for instance, at mortgage broker Charcol. **Moneyextra.com** *also has a tool allowing you to compare the various products on offer.*

One important decision you will have to make is choosing between a fixed rate mortgage or one which has variable rates. At present, interest rates may seem pretty low compared with the early 1990s, when they leapt to more than 12 per cent. You might think the 7 per cent level commonly quoted is much cheaper, but you have to consider real interest rates as well.

To do this, look at the current rate of inflation and subtract it from the headline interest rate. In the early 1990s, inflation hit almost 10 per cent. So real interest rates were approximately 2 per cent, At the time of writing in January 2000, inflation is at about

2 per cent: so real interest rates are 4 per cent: double what they were in the early 1990s! This means fixed rates may not be as good as they seem. After all, interest rates are far lower in Europe, and if we join the euro our rates will fall as well.

Mortgage providers have to borrow their money in turn, and in the UK they can't secure borrowing much below 4 per cent. This means they can't afford to lower interest rates on their mortgages to much below 5 per cent at present, so it may still be worth fixing your mortgage at this level if you can. Just be careful and shop around before committing yourself to anything.

If you are taking out a mortgage for the first time, explore the possibility of starter mortgages. These offer preferential rates for first-timers for a limited period. As always, check how beneficial this will be in the long run. Remember you will probably have to hold the mortgage for longer than just the lifetime of the introductory deal. Compare the rates the lender charges on its conventional products. That is the pattern your mortgage will conform to sooner or later.

Now before you go and plead with your landlord to take you back, scrunching up your mortgage agreement on your way over, there are ways of paying this sum off alongside paying off the interest. The most common method of doing this is via a repayment plan. In this type of mortgage you repay the capital sum as you pay off the interest. Using the same 8.65 per cent rate, this works out at £815 per month over twenty-five years. It seems strange that this is only £116 more than if you were just paying off the interest. However, since you are paying off a little of the capital sum each month, this outstanding amount is reduced at the same time; and as the twenty-five years progress, the interest on the sum falls equivalently. Over the whole period you end up paying only £144,608 in interest. So to buy the £100,000 flat will cost you £244,608 in all via this method.

An average interest rate of 8.65 per cent is less than that charged on most other loans. Banks charge more on overdrafts. And unsecured loans to buy cars are almost double this rate at the time of writing. If you think you will need to borrow in the future, there is another type of mortgage, only recently introduced, that could prove even more Foolish than a straight and inflexible repayment one.

One example is the Virgin One account. This, and other accounts like it, merge your mortgage borrowings with your current account. This means that your earnings are paid into and your monthly mortgage payments are taken out of the same place. What's the use of that, you might ask? Well, refer back to the first two chapters, when we discussed debt and saving money. Remember how we compared the interest rates you pay on debts with those you could expect to receive on savings. The ones on debts always easily outstripped those you could earn on savings. This is how banks and other financiers make money. Well, by paying your total monthly income into an account with your mortgage provider, you yourself can decide how much of your mortgage you can afford to pay off, depending on the other demands on your wallet that month. If you have lots of bills, you could even choose to pay none of your mortgage in certain exceptional months, as long as the amount outstanding is less than 95 per cent of the current value of the property. Your mortgage provider will merely charge interest monthly on the total outstanding amount. The only proviso is that the original debt is cleared by the time you retire, since by then you will no longer be paid a regular monthly salary. This flexible method allows you to borrow money for, say, holidays, a new car or even to pay little Johnny's school fees.

Getting interesting ...

The other main method of paying off the capital sum is to pay off the interest only each month, as we did above. And then, rather than repaying a little of the capital each month, you invest a fixed sum elsewhere to raise enough money to repay the capital sum in one go at the end of the period, when you have finished paying interest.

Take that £100,000 flat in South London again. As we worked out above, this sum will accrue £216,250 in interest at 8.65 per cent over twenty-five years, if you take out a full mortgage. You will have paid out an average of £699 a month to cover the interest payments on the £100,000 sum. In order to pay off the outstanding capital sum of £100,000, you will have to save money each month on top of your regular £699 payment. Now if this extra money didn't grow at all, you would have to pay in £333.33 each month to cover repayment of the £100,000 capital sum. Paying off £1,032.33 a month for twenty-five years would hardly be worth it because, as we have discovered, you could pay off £815 each month via a repayment mortgage, and guarantee to pay off the loan at the end of the period.

But just as the average interest rate on a mortgage can be calculated from the end of the Second World War, fifty years ago, so the average return from investing in the largest companies in the stock market has been calculated since the end of the First World War, more than eighty years ago. This long-term return works out at 12.2 per cent each year, according to the Barclays Capital Gilt Equity Study, of which more later. Via an index tracker, which rigidly follows the performance of such companies, individuals like you or me can drip in certain amounts each month and enjoy impressive annual returns such as these. This exercise can be accomplished reasonably cheaply as well. The best fund providers charge only 0.5 per cent annually, and tracker error can sometimes make the returns 0.3 per cent less than they should be.

So let's say the average long-term return per year from investing via this cheap and simple index-tracking method, which will be covered in more detail in Chapter Seven, is 11.4 per cent. Invest the £116 surplus you would have by choosing the interest-only rather than repayment mortgage route, and after twenty-five years this would give you £139,412. (This has been worked out using the compound interest formula in Chapter One. You will invest £1,392 every year over twenty-five years, at the rate of 11.4 per cent.)

Fast-forward twenty-five years and with this sum, you will now be able to pay off the £100,000 you owe easily, and have a surplus of £39,412 to do with as you wish. Of course this is just one example. All depends on the individual circumstances of your loan:

how long it lasts for, when repayment is due and the particular terms set by the mortgage company. Nevertheless this method is worth exploring over the traditional repayment system.

Beware of endowments

If you do decide to go down this path, be very wary of something called an endowment mortgage. This is an interest-only mortgage, in which the mortgage provider decides to invest your money in very complicated and expensive investment vehicles. These beasts are very inflexible and the complete opposite of cheap and simple index trackers. The investment plans commonly charge annual rates of 5 per cent or more, as well as various other fees for finishing the policy early. Compare this with the average index-tracking charge of 0.5 per cent, a tenth of the price.

More galling still is that 90 per cent of these expensive endowment funds, which are managed by Wise investment managers, have failed to beat the average market return mimicked by index trackers over the past five, ten and twenty-five years. Quite incredible. This means that if you are investing in one of these expensive and poor-performing plans, you will probably have to top up your monthly payments, because when the twenty-five years are up and you have to repay the mortgage, you may have insufficient funds and a shortfall to cover. Worrying.

The worst thing is that if this appears to be the case, you will probably be charged if you want to take your funds out of the endowment and switch to an alternative index tracker. This might mean it is not worth swapping because it is too costly. This leaves you with just one option: to continue to pay into the poorly performing endowment. No wonder the Wise want you to take one out, because once you have done so you are effectively trapped into paying them funds.

The Foolish lesson of this salutary tale is to avoid endowment plans at all costs at the outset. Even the Financial Services Authority has cottoned on to this favourite Wise trick and has issued a statement, warning insurance firms that sell endowments to make 'radical improvements … in communications with the estimated five million households which have mortgage endowments.' The regulator believes 'it is essential that better information in clear language is provided to customers about their position and their options for the future.'

So be Foolish, choose a cheap index-tracking plan if you opt for an interest-only mortgage. Or, if you will feel happier, stick to a simple repayment plan, but consider an all-in-one current account to make the most of your earnings and ease repayments by making them flexible. Above all, be careful and questioning before agreeing to taking on so much debt.

Conclusion

After all this complicated stuff, you may feel more comfortable sticking to renting. But before you do so, consider the one advantage of all this mortgage madness. At the end of the twenty-five-year term, you will own your own piece of capital: the South London flat. Now has it all been worth it? Say you opted to buy the flat, worth £100,000 at the outset, using a simple repayment mortgage. This means that, in effect, the flat would have cost you £244,608, assuming interest rates remain consistant. To make the whole thing worthwhile, you would want the flat to have appreciated in value by £144,608 once you have repaid the mortgage. This is 144.6 per cent over the twenty-five years, or roughly 5.8 per cent per year. Since 1945, property prices have increased by an average of 8.5 per cent each year, according to the Anglia House Price Survey. But interest rates have fluctuated dramatically. So the purchase, in this instance, would have been worthwhile.

Renting, on the other hand, may seem simpler in the short term, but if property prices continue to improve at the same rate there may be some benefit from buying a property. You will not gain a capital return from merely renting a place. But instead you could use your surplus cash to invest elsewhere, which, as we have touched on, could provide annual average returns of 12.5 per cent.

Having cleared highly rated debt off your back, found a roof over your head, put some pay in your pocket and got some cash in hand, you are now prepared to invest. Well done, Fool! Now follow me across the threshold to learn about planning for your future.

'Living together', living with lodgers and 'buying to let'

Whether you decide to live with your loved one, just with friends or even go as far as getting lodgers in to help pay your mortgage or the rent, remember this is a monetary arrangement as much as anything else. It's worth agreeing the exact terms and writing them down with the people you agree to live with, before actually going about it.

This isn't meant to sound harsh, but just a precaution in case anything goes wrong. After all, we are talking about quite substantial sums of money. You might think when the idea first arose that nothing could go wrong because you're so happy together, or because it's your best mate who's moving in. Try raising a smile just as broad six months down the track, when you're still waiting for two months' rent from your erstwhile best friend!

Your mortgage provider may not be as accommodating as you are, either. This brings us on to the scary scenario of buy-to-let mortgages. Tread very warily if you are contemplating capitalizing on the so-called property boom in this manner. By effectively taking out two mortgages, you have to get in lodgers as a mini-landlord. There are no two ways about it.

Any problems with this revenue stream and you could lose your whole 'investment'. Also, if interest rates move up rapidly then you will find things very painful, just as you will if rental rates drop severely. In short, be very careful with such schemes. You have little control over the revenue, and unless you have no mortgage liabilities then avoid them. In any case you can get better returns for your investment elsewhere, as we shall shortly reveal.

Ten Foolish steps up to your front door

1. We all need to live somewhere. You could stay with your parents. The other options are renting or buying a place.
2. Find somewhere you would be happy to stay, even if your situation changed. Mortgages are like marriages – hard to get out of once you are committed.
3. Renting is far more flexible than buying. It allows you to move at short notice.
4. Check the lease before signing it. Confirm basic terms such as rent, length of lease, notice periods, inventory and basic ground rules to avoid misunderstandings later on.
5. Buying a house is the biggest investment most people ever make. Consider what this means before taking the plunge. Rather than thinking of it as an investment, consider it primarily a place to live.
6. Repayment mortgages, as the name suggests, allow you to pay back the sum you have borrowed gradually over the lifetime of the loan at the same time as giving back interest payments.
7. Interest-only mortgages mean you only have to pay back the interest on the loan each month. You must pay back the capital sum borrowed at the end of the period.
8. Beware of using endowments to pay back mortgage capital. Most charge huge up-front fees and under-perform other investments substantially.
9. Two Foolish alternatives are using an index-tracking ISA-backed mortgage instead or setting up a flexible repayment mortgage account such as that provided by Virgin One.
10. Make sure you set out the financial obligations, before taking in a lodger or agreeing to cohabit. Be very wary of buy-to-let schemes. This is shorthand for doubling your mortgage borrowing.

Interlude: *Who wants to be a millionaire?*

(I don't! I don't!)

So far, all this turgid talk about scrimping together some cash to invest may have had you biting at the leash, desperate to get your investment life under way. But as I'm sure you'll now appreciate, it's far more Foolish to build a solid platform for your investments throughout your life than to start off on shifting sands.

But now it's time for ice cream. Well, not literally, but certainly it's our intermission break. If you want some light relief, now's the time to put the book down for a moment and rush off to get that drink. If you really want to you can turn to Chapter Five, where we get slightly more serious again. Hopefully, however, you'll stay with us.

I thought you might like to hear about how much better you're doing than two people who were in the lucky position of having money to invest, but who fell into Wise traps and completely and spectacularly failed to have any success at all. One is a pools winner and another a would-be French king. Sit back and savour these salutary tales.

Viv and the Pools

Back in the days when the National Lottery wasn't even a twinkle in the Government's eye, everyone dreamt of winning the Football Pools. This was an infinitely superior game. Rather than randomly picking six numbered balls from a total of forty-nine, players had to predict eight football matches, out of the sixty or so taking place each Saturday, that would end as a draw.

In other words, the aim was to choose the games where the sides scored one goal each, two goals each or more.

Experienced football fans could pretend they knew which games were more likely to end in draws. Other games, or 'permutations', could be played as well. Combinations of home wins, goal-less draws, even, in recent times, half-time scores: all could be predicted. In fact, addicts could even keep up their gambling hobby in the summer by following the weirdly named Australian soccer teams. Every newspaper worth its salt had a top tipster, writing a column or two each week. But this mattered little to most people, because easily the most popular aim was to win the jackpot by correctly picking the eight score draws on the Pools coupon, in a week when there were only eight score draws in all.

One Saturday in 1961, this dream of winning financial security through a simple game of chance came true for a housewife called Viv Nicholson. She won the enormous sum of £152,319. It might not sound like much today – in fact it could barely buy you a one-bedroom flat in Chelsea. But in the early 1960s it would have been enough to purchase a magnificent pile in the country with a hundred acres or so, as well as a town house in Belgravia. Assuming an inflation rate of 6 per cent, Viv's winnings were worth a staggering £1.4 million in modern money. A pint of beer in 1961 cost ten times less than it does today. A drink would cost only a few shillings, or less than ten new pence. And a pound would make you very happy indeed. With over 150,000 pieces of happiness, Viv thought she would never have to worry about money again, not surprisingly. Picking up her cheque, she told the envious reporters she intended to 'spend, spend, spend'. And boy, did she do that well.

She managed to get through five husbands, numerous fast cars, gallons of drink, and buckets of cash. Within a decade or so she had spent all she had won and was declared bankrupt. That's quite amazing. Now she hopes that the royalties from a new West End musical, based on her sorry tale, will help to make her financially solvent again.

However, Viv could have made herself and her children financially safe for the rest of her own and her grandchildren's lives with her windfall. A series of very simple investments, and a few relatively easy decisions about which ones to follow, would have made her capital sum watertight and still given her plenty to spend as she pleased.

Say, for example, she had used £100,000 to buy shares in the top thirty UK companies listed on the London Stock Exchange in 1961. If she had moved the shares as the top thirty companies changed – as some fell out of the table and others moved in to take their place – that £100,000 would now be worth £4.1 million.

If she had then put the remaining £50,000 in government-backed bonds called gilts, which can be bought over the counter at the Post Office and, like National Savings accounts, provide safe guaranteed returns, this would have given Viv an income of about £5,000 in 1961, rising to £45,000 today. Quite sufficient for a pleasant lifestyle, I'm sure you'd agree.

If someone with immense riches like Viv can end up spending it all, think how much easier it is for those of us with less money, or none at all, to do so! But instead, if we can curb our profligacy a little and salt away some cash into simple savings and investments schemes, we should be able to watch our money grow as quickly as Viv's pile dwindled.

A simple start might be to give up the Lottery and the vain attempt to pick six magic balls that will make you a millionaire. Let's take a look at the odds. There is only one chance in nearly *fourteen million* that your numbers will come up. Considering the population of the entire planet has only just passed six billion, it's surprising that rollover weeks, when no one wins the draw, don't happen more often!

In any case, in the unlikely event of you hitting the jackpot, winning windfall riches by chance can still mean you land up poor, perhaps bankrupt and even worse off than when you started, unless you have an investment plan – as the sorry tale of Viv Nicholson shows. And yet on average, 67 per cent of us play the National Lottery at least once a month. That's almost thirty million people. Yet only 830 individual millionaires have been created so far, or 0.002 per cent of the regular players. More frightening still is that last year, each of those regular players spent an average of £43 on the Lottery. Invest that money regularly elsewhere, and you will be far more likely to reach millionaire status in the long run.

Live like a king?

In the summer of 1999, the pretender to the French throne died. Henri d'Orleans, Comte de Paris, was a direct descendant of the last king of France, Louis Philippe, who fled the country in 1848. If the monarchy had survived, Henri would have been Henri VI of France. However, although he didn't manage to inherit the throne, he was still left a £400 million fortune by his father in 1940, as the head of the House of Orleans.

But in turn, the would-be king left his descendants just six handkerchiefs and a pair of slippers. One of Henri's nine children is preparing a legal action following the publication of his will. The lawyer leading the action said that he had failed to recover any of the family's heirlooms and that all Henri's bank accounts were left empty. He suggests that Henri may have hidden the assets in secret locations in an effort to disinherit his children, who he had fallen out with. Yet others believe that the pretender had in fact squandered his immense pile on gambling and other reckless pursuits. Certainly over the last twenty-five years Henri had sold all his numerous manors, chateaux and estates. By the time he died, the ninety-year-old head of the family lived in a modest bungalow owned by his mistress. Other luxury goods such as antiques and jewellery, including some diamonds that had belonged to Marie Antoinette, had also been sold, at ludicrously low prices.

Heir Jacques d'Orleans' lawyer said he thought it was impossible for his client's father to have spent all the 100 million francs he is estimated to have raised from this selling spree. 'Maybe the man had a hatred of his children,' he said. 'Maybe he just went mad towards the end of his life.' The investigation is under way, but Foolish lessons can be learnt from this staggering story, particularly if it turns out that Henri's royal investment touch really did desert him.

To turn £400 million into £40, or lose 99.99 per cent of this fortune over a fifty-nine-year period when inflation has been roaring, is almost unbelievable. The only possible way Henri's actions could be deemed Foolish is if he had decided that his assets were too heavily concentrated in the French property market, and in illiquid items like antiques, paintings, diamonds and jewellery. In recent years the underlying prices of diamonds and precious metals like gold have been dropping disastrously as deflation rears its ugly head again.

A Fool could understand it if he had been desperate to get involved in equities, and had switched from commodities to shares. The French stock market has boomed lately. Over the past ten years the CAC 40 index of leading shares on the Paris bourse has risen 181.2 per cent. Thus if Henri had put his £400 million in a fund tracking this index, he would have left his family over £1,124.8 million. With the throne gone, this may not have been enough to restore the fortunes of the House of Orleans completely, but it would have prevented his children from having to go out to work (poor devils!).

In 1940 £400 million would have probably bought most companies in London's FT 30 index of the thirty leading UK companies, in their entirety. However, imagine Henri had escaped at Dunkirk with the Free French but had only managed to bring over £40 (the sum he has left his descendants). At that time, the FT 30 had plunged to an all-time low of 49.4, as more pressing concerns, such as the raging war, occupied most inhabitants of the Allied countries. However, if carefree Henri had decided to put just this £40 on the FT 30, today he would be sitting on a remarkable £3.24 million. Over the past fifty-nine years, this blue chip index has increased by 8003.8 per cent.

Many more Foolish investors could have replicated this with such a long-term buy and hold strategy. Indeed, a recent survey suggests that many British people have started saving for the long term to some degree. In a report funded by the Joseph Rowntree Foundation, the Policy Studies Institute found that those who have recently retired are the richest group in the country. The average wealth of sixty- to sixty-nine-year-olds is now £133,000. The survey puts this down to assets from pension funds, the increasing number of homeowners and increased benefit provision.

More worrying, though, were those people interviewed who were scared about being poor in retirement, but were either not bothered or didn't feel compelled to save for the future. The report concluded that recent Government proposals, including the stakeholder pension scheme, 'makes it less likely that people will save the sort of sums that would provide them with the retirement income to which they aspire'.

However, if you are feeling poor and want to start getting exposure to equities Foolishly, then read on and you might get some idea how to avoid 'King' Henri's fate. We are going to tell you all about how to start investing directly in shares with small amounts of money, without using managed schemes or brokers. This is via dividend reinvestment plans or DRiPs, which are run by large companies. Skip to Chapter Eight for more information. If you follow these simple schemes over the long term, you will be hard pressed to lose as much as Henri. In fact it is more likely that you will become the King of France than replicate Henri's 99.99 per cent losses!

And now please put down your popcorn, as it's time to return to tonight's main Foolish feature … !

Chapter Five – The pension problem

Ah, were I courageous enough
To shout, Stuff your pension!
But I know, all too well, that's the stuff
That dreams are made on.
Philip Larkin, 'Toads'

What money problem scares people the most? The majority would say the prospect of penury in old age. This is why lots of us want to save, to avoid this unfortunate fate. Many investors' principal aim is to provide themselves with an income in retirement when they can no longer earn a salary, or of course don't wish to do so any more.

To satisfy this end, one of the first things a lot of people do is explore the possibility of paying into a pension. This, though, can prove to be the worst way of achieving the simple objective of finding retirement income. Well, that's not entirely true. There is one action that is even worse: you could simply save nothing at all and rack up debts instead.

Faced with this situation, let us take Alexander Pope's proverb, 'Fools rush in where angels fear to tread,' and turn it on its head. In this instance, the truly Foolish move is to assess all your options angelically, before alighting on a particular course of action. So rather than signing up for any old pension plan provided by your employer or anyone else, stand back for a while and wonder why you are scared.

Who has filled you with such fear? You may not be surprised to hear, having got this far, that there is an alarmist agenda being set by a Wise committee out there. (Well not really, but it certainly seems as if there might be a conspiracy.) You have probably picked up the heebie-jeebies from either a Government spokesman or a representative of a financial services firm. Such Wise guys have no doubt impressed upon you the need to start saving for a pension as soon as possible. Frightening facts about the need to build a pension pot have no doubt come flying your way in newspapers, now that the basic state pension, currently worth a paltry £66.75 a week, looks set to dwindle even further. On the other hand you may remember that personal pensions, the alternative to state and company provision, are not too highly thought of either, what with many being 'mis-sold' to investors in the early 1990s.

Despite this blinding problem, most people will still plant their money in a regular scheme run by a Wise finance provider. Why? Because such firms specialize in scaring you, to make it easier for them to spirit your money away to supposed safety. They convince you by reassuring you of their sure-footedness and reliability as well as of their ability to achieve these aims. With a pat on your head, you are told not to worry about a thing and sit back, contribute monthly and wait placidly for a pay-out when you hit the jackpot age of sixty-five. But always remember that the seemingly mild-mannered people selling this idyll are working for the same firms accused of mis-selling such products. Contradiction or what?

Before you join the headlong lemming rush to hand over control of your money to such 'professionals', perhaps you should question why so many people are considering following this Wise move. Is it because they feel there are no alternatives?

Well, don't worry, there are ways and means of reaching happiness on your own, without the 'help' of such salesmen. All these multifarious and fabulously Foolish options will be revealed in this and the following chapters. Just remember as you read that at the end of the day, it's up to you to look at the alternatives and decide upon your own course of action, depending on your own particular circumstances, attitudes to risk and other matters. Check out what is on offer, and don't do anything unless you are certain it is suitable for you. And above all keep your Foolish wits about you. Don't let anyone, Wise or otherwise, pull wool over your Foolish eyes.

Be very wary if you are offered unsolicited advice about a pension. Anybody who wants to sell you a pension does not primarily have your interests at heart. His first aim is to secure his own living through commission. He's not just doing this for fun or because he loves his job. His principal aim, I suggest, is quite naturally to make as much money as possible. Paying fees to advisers who are not reliant on selling high-commission products is a better option; but best of all, and most Foolish, is to work out, *yourself*, what options exist for providing you with retirement income. However, you don't have to undertake this task entirely alone.

Many Fools on the Motley Fool Web site's *Pensions* and *Endowments* boards (**boards.fool.co.uk**) have revealed some of the worst tactics pension salesmen have used against them. One particular firm has come in for a lot of abuse. This is because of its practice of urging its sales representatives to approach their own acquaintances with awful pension proposals. It must be awful to commit commission-based selling sins on your supposed 'friends'. I urge you to look at the section later in this chapter for details. And take a look at the contributions on these message boards, and learn from other Fools' experiences when dealing with pension providers. If you have any specific queries or uncertainties about your proposed plans, why not post them on the board? I'm sure you will find the responses from fellow Fools both illuminating and reassuring. (That's another reason to get online! How many more reasons do you need?)

Wise up to the Wise!

If you read Chapter Four on house buying, you will remember the Foolish warning about buying endowment policies to pay off mortgages. If not, go and sneak a look now. It's only a few pages back. You may recall there were three essential Foolish complaints about these ultra-Wise products. First of all, they were very expensive. Secondly, they were purposely made incredibly complicated to understand. And thirdly, most underperformed rival products by quite a significant margin.

At the Fool, we lump pensions together with endowments as the Wisest of Wise financial products. Both betray poor individual investors in the ways outlined above. Yet providers of such beasts attempt to disguise this expensive underperformance, dressing it up in very Wise language, via many methods, because this is where they generate significant amounts of ill-gotten commission. That's why Fools have so little time for them both, and talk about them in the same breath on the Motley Fool message boards when warning others of the traps unsuspecting souls can fall into. At heart, the basic premise of both pensions and endowments is the same.

For a fee, normally amounting to on average 5 per cent of the sum you put into the fund each year as well as a significant amount (2 per cent) of all the planned contributions, a professional will manage the money you give him to look after. He will place it where he can and invest it on your behalf. This pot should build up cumulatively, until on maturity he returns it to you to do with as you will. The endowment policy is intended to pay off the mortgage initially loaned to you. Most of the pension pot has to be spent, when you retire, on buying an annuity from a life assurance company. This annuity will give you an income for life, as determined by interest rates at the time. If you die only a few years after buying your annuity, the life assurance firm pockets the remaining money. Tough!

The problem is that by docking 5 per cent off your funds each year, and in some cases 2 per cent off all the funds you plan to contribute to the policy (known as an initial fee), you have less money working for you to start with than if you invested it yourself. Also, the Wise fund will have to perform 5 per cent better, since under a Wise scheme your cash automatically starts 5 per cent behind money invested Foolishly. There are simple tried and tested methods that you can use, which are far cheaper. For now, just remember that for every £100 invested Foolishly, you will only have £95 working for you Wisely.

The other big drawback of such Wise policies is that very few consistently manage to match – let alone beat – the market average, or benchmark, return, even before fees and charges are accounted for. In fact 90 per cent of funds have failed to beat the performance of the FTSE 100 group of leading shares on the stock market over the past five, ten or twenty-five years. Staggering, then, that so many misguided individuals continue to put their hard-earned money into such miserable and high-charging funds.

Perhaps people feel that there are no alternatives, and that using a Wise provider of a complicated, expensive and underperforming policy is the only way to invest small sums in the market. Since pension funds account for over a third of the funds currently invested in the UK stock market, this would appear to be the case. Another factor may be the not ungenerous tax breaks given by the Government, which are used to woo investors into parting with their cash and putting it into pension funds. Company pension schemes also offer incentives, such as the company matching its employees' contributions, or at least contributing a little towards this sum.

As ever, you should work out your own particular circumstances and weigh up your options before plunging in. But remember that no amount of perks from the Inland Revenue or Your Employer plc can disguise the expensive fees of pension fund providers, and the poor performance of their funds. Well, not *their* funds of course, but the funds they manage terribly for poor, downtrodden individual pension savers, who have given control of their savings to the Wise.

Remember, time is on your side. Better to spend a few days, or even weeks, working out your various options, rather than rushing into any expensive plan offered by a Wise provider. Over the long run, a few weeks will not make as much difference to the eventual outcome of your investments as a detrimental decision, made snappily, to put your money in a poorly performing fund that charges very expensive initial charges and considerable ongoing annual fees.

Are Independent Financial Advisers really 'Independent'?

We've already warned you several times about the drawbacks of using Wise investment schemes, and particularly about the expensive fees that many charge for their underperforming vehicles. Perhaps, then, you have considered seeking 'independent' advice from an independent financial adviser, commonly known as an IFA.

Be very careful when consulting such advisers. This might seem strange, as normally you are told by advertisers of financial products to seek independent financial advice. We applaud this idea in principle, since it is very Foolish to look at every option and assess any product independently before buying it.

But IFAs don't offer this option. No, unfortunately, IFAs are in league with the Wise. They have hijacked the word 'independent' and bastardized it. You may wonder, if you have a free consultation with an IFA, how he makes his money. Just ask yourself, or even better, ask the IFA. He picks up a certain percentage of the commission fees you are charged by the Wise fund provider. This means it is in his financial interest to lead you towards the products that charge the most commission, since this will in turn enhance his own income. Whoa, that's not very independent, you might think. And you'd be right.

That's why, if you do decide to use an IFA, you should go only to one who explicitly states that he, or she, will charge you a fee up front at an hourly rate, rather than one who is reliant on recouping commission and gives you the 'gift' of a free consultation. Nevertheless, IFAs are human, and will probably try to steer you to the high commission products anyway, to get more money for themselves.

So even better is to get a fee-based IFA who pays back any commission he earns from selling you a product. But be careful and treat IFAs like the second-hand car salesmen they mostly are. In any case, if you have limited funds as a novice investor, you will probably baulk at the prospect of paying for financial advice up front. Don't worry though, you don't have to! Instead, get some free opinions from fellow Foolish consumers on the Motley Fool's message boards. Foolish contributors may be biased, but they are speaking from real experience of having used such rubbish products and,

moreover, are not disguising the fact that they are not independent.
They are unashamedly Foolish!

There are cheap alternatives available, which do at least match
the market and in many cases outperform it. By saving a little
each month you can build up significant sums by compounding
returns, without giving a lot of your money in charges to
professionals who fail to do their job properly. Remind yourself
of the beauteous miracle of compound interest mentioned
earlier. But before we come on to these wonderfully Foolish
ideas, let's first look in more detail at the pension options
currently available.

The basic state pension

Perhaps the bands of the 1960s, such as The Who, were more
forward-thinking than people usually give them credit for when
they suggested that they wanted to die before they got old.
Seeing the current impecunious state of old age pensioners, you
might think that The Who, by advocating early death, were in
fact visionary prophets. Tragically, though, lots of pop idols
followed this advice to the letter. Jimi Hendrix, Janis Joplin, Jim
Morrison, John Lennon and, more recently, Kurt Cobain all left
the world's stage early. Even The Who's very own drummer,
Keith Moon, bowed out in his prime. (Incidentally, why did so
many pop stars to suffer early deaths have a first name beginning
with the letter J? Creepy.)

The baby-boom generation, who were teenagers in the
1960s, took this gospel on board. Amidst all the high living and
high jinks, it was unlikely that many of these groovy chicks and
fellers gave any thought to their old age, let alone their pensions.
This was partly because there wasn't a lot to discuss. This was the
era when there was still virtually full employment. Thinking
about how they would provide for themselves in the 'uncool'
grey town of retirement-ville never occurred to anyone. After all,
the Welfare State was still in fine fettle. The old age pension,

provided by the Government, was sufficient for most people's needs. The grannies of many mods and rockers didn't seem too badly off. No one seemed to be going short. This was because the Government still provided an old age pension that moved up in line with average earnings, allowing the grey brigade to keep pace easily with modern spending patterns, if not with hip fashions.

However, Roger Daltrey and crew have now reached retirement age. Although they might be in a fine financial state themselves, living off the royalties from hits such as the rock opera *Tommy*, the picture for their contemporaries and many fans is not as rosy as it was for their elderly relatives thirty years ago.

In 1981, the Government severed the link between average earnings and the old age pension. Instead, state pensions now rise in line with prices, or in other words inflation. So what, you might say! Well back in 1981 you could expect to receive £29.60 a week as a pensioner. The average weekly wage was £125, so as an OAP you didn't feel too disadvantaged – you were receiving 24 per cent of what you would have done if you were still working. Since then, though, earnings have risen much faster than prices. Basic goods have become cheaper relative to wages, which have improved. And at the same time, money spent on luxurious living has exploded.

Remember, in Chapter One, how compounding different rates of interest produced dramatically varied returns after more than a few years? Well, since the Government applied this Foolish law almost twenty years ago, the basic state pension has gone up only 125 per cent to £66.75 a week, in line with slow-growing prices and inflation, whereas average weekly earnings have marched ahead more quickly, by more than three times, to £385. So the state pension is now worth just 17 per cent of earnings.

If this trend continues, as it looks likely to do, with inflation increasing more slowly than earnings, then in another thirty years the pension will only represent 10 per cent of average earnings. Rely on this pay-out alone and you are going to struggle once you hit retirement age. This barrier itself looks set to rise, too. The Government has already raised the pensionable age for women born after 1950, from sixty to sixty-five. Indeed, many other bodies looking into the tricky problem of pension provision reckon the Government should lift the official retirement age even higher, to, say, seventy.

In fact, this would be in line with the original aim of old age pensions. They were designed to alleviate poverty in the final few years of people's lives. When introduced by Lloyd George in the 1900s, life expectancy was about fifty. If you reached the end of your working life at sixty-five, you could only expect to live another few years. Most people worked until they dropped. Pensions were thus designed as an insurance measure against reaching old age, so that you had something to live off if you could no longer work. Hence the name for this plan: the National Insurance scheme.

Nowadays, people live longer. Someone hitting sixty-five can expect to survive for another twenty years. But pensions are still set up as insurance policies. Hence, as people live longer, the costs of servicing them are immense. So governments are shifting responsibility to the individual, and other pension providers are increasing their costs while sticking to the old insurance-based models.

What is needed is a radical change of thinking on the part of both prospective pensioners, that's you, me and everyone else under sixty-five, and pension providers – the Government and financial service providers. In fact we should not think in terms of pensions and retirement at all. People are already giving up their main source of work earlier than usual, from the age of fifty onwards. Yet many are still continuing to work part-time for another twenty years or more, until they are well into their seventies. This can be in either a monetary or a voluntary capacity. Such active types could hardly be called shy and retiring.

So instead of seeking an idle retirement, you should be looking for alternative forms of income when you are no longer working in a nine-to-five job. This could come from many sources. Do not rely on the promise of a pension to provide for you exclusively. And if you only have the state pension to rely on you may, I'm afraid, just have to 'hope you die before you get old …'

Before moving on to ways of solving this dilemma, I should just mention another state scheme called SERPS. This stands for state earnings-related pension scheme. As the name 'earnings-related' suggests, this method allows you to top up your basic state pension by increasing your National Insurance payments from your pay packet. However, as with the basic pension scheme, pay-outs have been dwindling for some time in real terms. And in any case you can only receive a maximum of £4,000 a year from SERPS. That works out at £77 a week.

You can contract out of these NI payments. Indeed the Government is encouraging this by offering rebates on previous contributions to SERPS. Contact the Department of Social Security at **www.dss.gov.uk** for more details. Nevertheless, you will still have to look further afield for a means of receiving income after the age of sixty-five.

Company pension plans

As mentioned in the chapter on work, few people nowadays will remain with just one employer for the forty years of their working life. Even fewer can expect an employer to provide them with an old-style pension. Sure, many companies entice their staff with the prospect of a company pension scheme. But this can mean all manner of things. The Government has made it possible for employers to offer a variety of different plans to their employees. No wonder, then, that there is such confusion.

The best old-style plans, the classics of their day, are like big game in Africa: still the leaders in their field but increasingly rare to spot. These beasts are called final salary schemes. Such schemes will pay you a certain amount each year from when you retire. As the name suggests, the amount depends on your final salary and how long you have worked for the company. The Wise call such plans defined-benefit schemes. This is because you, the beneficiary, will receive a defined amount throughout your retirement, based on the two criteria above. Effectively you are tied to one employer from when you start working until the day you die. The investment performance of the underlying fund matters not a jot to your retirement income, so whatever happens you are quids in. Fantastic, unless of course you are a fund manager underperforming the index – in which case you stand to lose significantly, particularly as the pensioners you are paying live longer.

More than two-thirds of company pensions still operate like this, but fewer new ones are being offered. They are becoming more unpopular, particularly with companies but also with employees, who are switching jobs more frequently and with greater ease. This means the number of years working for one company is correspondingly less and employees qualify for less retirement benefit.

A more common company scheme is called a money-purchase scheme. This will not guarantee you a particular pension pay-out. As with a personal pension or endowment, mentioned above, you contribute regular payments to a Wisely-managed fund, with its attendant drawbacks. When you retire you will have to use most of this pot to buy a beastly annuity from a Wise life assurance company. What might make such a scheme worthwhile, though, are contributions from your employer to the pension pot.

Stand back a moment. Take this in. In this instance someone is *giving* you money. Wow! Do you remember the thrill of opening an envelope on your birthday and a crisp fiver falling out? Exactly. No doubt you foamed at the mouth at the prospect of buying more stickers for your football album or more clothes for your dollies. Cash offerings can't be sniffed at, even if your employer is only contributing in lieu of services you have rendered him.

Focus on how generous he is really being. Do you think if you did the same work for another employer who had no pension scheme, you would be paid more to make up for this loss of pension income? Will your own employer allow you to have this money, destined for your company pension plan, in cash instead, so you can invest it Foolishly? He may not mind and it could prove cheaper for him. Explore such possibilities.

If you don't accept this gift, do you really think you'll be able to find the extra cash off your own back? The sacrifices may not be worth it if the contribution is a significant sum. However, if you do accept the money and join the pension plan, you will have very little choice as to where the money is invested. Rival professional pension fund managers will have put in bids for the mandate, or right, to manage your company's employee pension fund. Hang around, professional fund managers? Now where have we encountered these Wise devils before? That's right, these are the beggars with exorbitant fees and charges. And 90 per cent of them regularly fail to beat the FTSE 100 index of leading shares on the stockmarket.

Waoah! Bad isn't it? That's why you have to weigh up the benefits of employer contributions against the drawbacks of an expensive and poorly performing fund you have no choice over. Before agreeing to anything, Foolishly find out how the fund has performed, and what exactly the managers are investing in and why. After all, this is your money. And moreover, you are relying on this chappie in suit and tie for your fiscal happiness when you retire.

If you are unhappy with what you have found, e-mail your fellow employees pointing out your Foolish findings. Lobby to meet the trustees of the fund and get them to consider changing fund managers. And by all means post a question on the Motley Fool's message boards to gain insight from fellow Fools, who have experienced similar predicaments, as to how the fund is performing and the pros and cons of accepting a company pension scheme.

If this is all to no avail and you are stuck with what you've got, always keep tabs on what the fund expects your future pay-out to be. If you feel there will be a shortfall, look at organizing a more Foolish fund to fall back on. Do not top up contributions in the poorly performing fund. Do you really want to throw good money after bad?

Before moving on, you might want an explanation as to why such funds underperform. This is mainly because they are trying to achieve vastly different things for people at different stages of the cycle. The fund has to grow as quickly as possible for people in their twenties, thirties, forties and fifties. To do this it will invest in fast-growing stocks and shares. But at the same time, the fund has to pay out regular amounts to those who are retiring in their sixties, seventies, eighties and nineties. The fund therefore has to invest in income-producing instruments as well, such as bonds. Combining both strategies pulls down overall performance. This affects savers who can achieve a better return by running their own plans.

This is a conflict of interest which as an individual you can overcome by becoming much more efficient, and focusing all your investments in stocks and shares until you decide to take some income from them when you are no longer working. Then you can sell a small proportion as and when you need to, and invest, then and only then, in income-producing bonds or even some shares. More about you taking Foolish control will follow.

There is just one other Wise product connected with company pension schemes that you are best to approach with kid gloves. This is something very mysterious called the Additional Voluntary Contribution or AVC. As the name suggests, this scheme allows you to make extra payments into your company pension, on top of the standard package you have already organized. You can contribute up to 15 per cent of your salary no matter what age you are.

What's the benefit of that? Well, you can gain tax relief on these payments, as with all pension schemes, but you are still lumbered with your company pension plan's expensively managed fund. And remember, nine out of ten of them tend to underperform the market average. So instead of putting these extra savings into the same pension plan, you may be better off diversifying into something more Foolish.

Personal pension plans
When discussing company schemes we said that sometimes employers actually contribute to them. These gifts are made

before you are taxed; the pension is just another item to come off your gross salary. That's right: contributions to pension schemes are tax-free. This applies to personal pensions as well, although in this instance, since by definition personal pensions are not organized by your company, the Government will reimburse the tax you have already paid on your contributions. So say you are taxed at the basic rate of 23 per cent, giving you a take-home monthly salary of £1,000, net of taxes. If you then decide to put £77 a month into a personal pension fund, the Government will reimburse the £23 you have already paid in tax, giving you a total pension contribution of £100 per month.

This tax break is the basic allure of such schemes, particularly if you are in the higher tax bracket and pay income tax at 40 per cent. Then you only have to pay £60, and the Government tops it up to £100. Very Foolish! You might wonder why the Government is being so generous. This is most out of character! But part of their aim is to get you to save for your retirement, so that the state doesn't have to pick up the tab when you have frittered all your cash away.

Also, surprise, surprise, there are conditions connected to this generosity. First of all, you can only, until the age of thirty-six, put 17.5 per cent of your annual income into a pension. This rises to 20 per cent from thirty-six to forty-five; 25 per cent from forty-six to fifty; 30 per cent from fifty-one to fifty-five; 35 per cent from fifty-six to sixty; and 40 per cent from sixty-one to sixty-five. Moreover, all regular pay-outs from pension schemes, company or personal, are liable to income tax.

Yes, when you finally retire, you will have to pay tax on the regular income you receive from your pension. Naturally this works out best if you pay into a pension plan as a higher rate tax payer, and receive benefits from the plan as a basic rate tax payer. In that way you are already making a 17 per cent saving on the transaction before factoring in any growth at all.

This complicated tax system is not the only special condition surrounding personal pensions. As with company pensions, you have a limited choice as to where to invest your savings. Most personal pension schemes are run by very Wise financial firms, who offer you a limited range of their own expensive and underperforming funds. This allows them to rake in excessive fees. By hooking you with the juicy tax break, they can pretend the fund is actually performing well whereas in fact this is mostly the effect of the tax break.

And once you are with them you will find it hard to leave for another provider without incurring exorbitant charges. This scandalous and inflexible charging structure is why personal pensions have come in for such criticism by the Government, who have seen firms rake in fees at the expense of clients who would have been better off sticking with their company's pension scheme.

Even more worrying is that personal pensions offer an even smaller range of options as to how you receive the final pay-out. You can receive 25 per cent of the sum you have accumulated as a lump of cash to blow on a luxury cruise around the world, or reinvest Foolishly as you wish. You can take this sum at any time from the age of fifty-five onwards. But before you attain the massive age of seventy-five, you will have to use the remaining money in your pension pot to buy an annuity, as with a company pension plan.

An an-what-ity? Annuities are dreadful beasts that are sold exclusively by Wise insurance companies, the ones we have been warning you to treat very carefully. They guarantee a regular income for life, based on interest rates at the time you purchase the scheme and on the size of your pot. At the moment, with interest rates relatively low, people nearing retirement who are being forced to consider an annuity have gulped when they have seen the tiny income projections given by Wise insurers.

Annuities are like a gamble being taken out on the beneficiary's life. If you only live for a few years after you purchase the annuity, then don't expect your nearest and dearest, or the Hedgehog Hospital, to pick up the remaining proceeds. No, the Wise will keep the funds, thank you very much. In fact you're going to have to live at least ten years or more to make the whole process worth your financial while.

Worrying, isn't it? We at the Fool think that this requirement – to buy annuities with money saved in a pension vehicle – is so worrying that it should be overhauled. If you think so as well, then join us in a campaign to rectify this appalling situation. Write to your local MP, or send an e-mail to the Government or the Treasury at **public.enquiries@hm-treasury.gov.uk**. Perhaps post a message on the Fool's message boards (**boards.fool.co.uk**) so we can pass it on to the Government.

Maybe, if we're successful and persuade the Government to change the rules, the annuity requirement will have gone by the time you retire, and you can truly be Foolish with your money. Don't bet on it happening soon though, since the Government receives plenty of income from the tax payable on annuities. In the meantime, since you still have time on your side, there are alternatives you might like to follow.

Some pension horror stories from the Motley Fool message boards

One of the most active message boards on the Motley Fool Web site is the Pensions board. Many people post queries about their pensions, hoping Fools with similar experiences will be able to help them by offering ideas. The board has attracted several thousand messages and debates about Foolish pension options. This shows the level of concern this issue is causing at present.

Here are just a few messages posted over the past year, showing the type of real-life problems that pensions can create. Last June, a Fool called PJ Broke wrote:

'My son was advised to start a pension last year. He is only twenty and can only afford £50 a month. So, in all faith, he went to his local bank, the Midland. I have been abroad and have only just looked at the policy and it is criminal:

Year	Amount paid to date	Charges to date
1	655	352
2	1,309	556
3	1,964	669
4	2,618	791
5	3,273	924

After five years he will have been charged nearly a third of his payments. What should he do – cancel the policy?'

This isn't as bad as some other pension providers. Back in January another Foolish poster, Rachid, talked about supposedly 'independent' financial advice:

Dear Fools,
I would like to relate a little story, which began with a visit to an IFA salesman whose company sold me a pension plan some four years ago. The company had a change of personnel in the meantime.
I was appalled by the performance of the current pension fund, which on average returned less than 6 per cent annually – during a bull market. Unfortunately, at the time I did not know as much as I should have done about financial matters, and certainly did not have access to the excellent Motley Fool UK Investment Guide.
So, as I was not happy with the first pension plan, he proceeded to recommend a new plan which of course was front-loaded with a handsome commission to the IFA. I tackled him on this point (armed with my new knowledge) and he said he could offer a better plan if we were to proceed on a fee basis.
I refrained from getting angry at this point. I told him that I knew exactly what I wanted, which was basically to transfer the funds built up in the first plan into a low cost plan which did not have the ambition of beating the market, just matching it.
At that point he said, 'I would do the same if I were you.

However, I cannot endorse your action as my company would not agree with it.' (Loss of commission I guess!!) He then suggested, since I seemed to know quite a lot about it, that I handle all the paperwork on my own.

I felt a bit cheated at this point. The company, which this salesman works for, received £2,780 commission on the first plan. Now, instead of rectifying the matter, the salesman had the cheek to suggest that since I had not proceeded with his recommendation of opening a second plan with his company, I should still pay him a fee of £400 for the two hours he spent researching a plan for me.

I think this industry is really getting away with a lot. Does anybody get paid for preparing a quotation for potential work in the real competitive world out there? The answer is of course no, otherwise we would all be rich from going around quoting! Thanks for making me a happy Fool. Happy New Year to all of you.

Rachid

And finally Sean J told Fools about his sad brush with the pension industry:

I first got interested in Foolish finance when I picked up a copy of the original book in the US. I'm now reading the (excellent) UK Investment Guide. *I have reread the thrilling section on the power of compound interest.*

I smiled smugly when I read about fools who left investing till their thirties, rather than the Fools who started early. Me? I started my first pension when I was still a student. I put £50 a month into a policy with a Scottish company. £50 was all I could afford. It meant going WITHOUT BEER at times.

Since then I have started two other pensions. They get the bigger contributions. The Scottish company kept receiving my £50.

I decided to check out the growth of my fund having carefully put each yearly statement directly into a filing cabinet without looking at it.

From 1991 to 1997 I had made £3,600 in contributions. Coinciding with the greatest bull market in history, the value of my fund was … £3,685.

I also noted that £3.40 was being deducted from every £50 contribution.

This unnerved me. I checked out the figures on my other pensions. One seemed to have done well. As for the other, I had made £4,500 in contributions. It had been arranged by a nice IFA about whom we subsequently received a letter, saying that if we knew where he was could we tell his former employers and/or the Police!

Having been contributing for only three and a half years, I was not expecting to see much, if any, real growth. This was good, because my fund was worth £3,700 in August 1998, showing an £800 loss. It turns out that I had taken out a combined pension and life assurance policy (had I?!) The statements record the value of contributions and the value of the fund, but nowhere tell you how much has been funnelled off into the life assurance contributions.

Now I comfort myself that 40 per cent of these contributions have, in effect, been made by the Inland Revenue. However I have learned some lessons:

Charges really do matter and whatever your IFA may say (on the phone from Wormwood Scrubs), they are not all 'much the same'.

Just because money is leaving your account monthly does not mean you are secure. Check what is happening to your money.

Sean

And as an encore, consider this contribution by another Fool, David Carter, last May. He quotes from the letter he received from his Wise pension provider in reply to a query about his pension:

'Reduced Allocation Period (RAP)
During this period we used 35 per cent of your regular contribution to buy units in your chosen fund(s) and the remainder to cover the costs of setting up your plan or each new investment level to it.'

For those Fools who aren't aware of my previous gripe, the 'each new investment level to it' refers to any increased contribution paid into the account. So when the salesperson talks you into parting with another £100 per month, only £35 of the new money goes into the *investment. Shocked? Read on!*

"The RAP varies according to the length of the Contribution Payment Term (CPT), which is the time you've agreed to pay into the plan for. The RAP will apply for the same number of months as the CPT is in years, up to a maximum of thirty months. For your plan, the CPT is twenty-three years, the RAP is twenty-three months."

Oh, I see. So for twenty-three months at the start of the pension, and then for twenty-three months after each successive increase, your charges are a mere 65 per cent. Perfectly clear so far, and ten out of ten for not trying to hide that fact.

"Once the RAP has expired, we will buy regular contributions at 105 per cent for the remainder of the CPT. However, we've started your plan by using the preferential terms transfer, which means that we enhance the allocation on contributions up to the previous amounts you've paid. So, for the first £43.50 of your monthly contribution, we've allocated 83.76 per cent to purchase units for the first twenty-three months of the plan. We've allocated the remaining £56.50 at 35 per cent for twenty-three months. This included all contributions to 1 December 1997, after which we allocated the contributions we received at 105 per cent to units."

I think this means they feel a little guilty at fleecing me up front, and therefore pay a bit back and call it 105 per cent to make it sound like I'm getting more than I'm paying in. They've lost me a bit here.'

In all, David worked out that the contributions of £6,000 he had paid in were now worth a little over £4,000. Worrying indeed. If you have any questions of your own please contribute them to the ongoing debate on the Motley Fool's Pensions board. Many thanks to all these Fools for their haunting messages.

Ten Foolish pension posers to consider before enrolling in a Wise scheme:

1. Don't rush into taking out a pension. Check out all the options available to you.

2. Ask yourself who has made you worry about the prospect of penury in old age: was it a Wise institution or the Government?

3. Wise up to the Wise! The main aim of many Wise professional pension salesmen is to make as much commission as possible rather than to give you the best deal. Take a look at the Motley Fool's message boards for confirmation of this point.

4. This makes the products they sell expensive and incredibly complicated to understand. Many have also significantly underperformed the market average, even before such charges are included.

5. Are Independent Financial Advisers really independent? Only no-commission fee-based ones might be.

6. The basic state pension is a miserly £66.75 a week and is decreasing in relative spending power. You'll have to look elsewhere for retirement bliss.

7. Company pension schemes are disguised Wise plans. Final salary schemes are the best but are becoming less popular. Money purchase schemes are less generous, unless your employer contributes money to the scheme. This is a gift and will be hard to turn down.

8. Be wary of personal pension plans. Look out for the outrageous charges many carry.

9. Write a letter to the Treasury to ask for the requirement for pensions to buy annuities to be lifted.

10. Don't be deceived by the tax breaks pension contributions receive. Any eventual proceeds from a pension are taxed at the normal rates. This can outweigh any up-front benefits tax breaks on contributions give you.

Chapter Six – The Foolish alternative to pensions

'Who cares for you?' said Alice (she had grown to her full size by this time). 'You're nothing but a pack of cards!'
Lewis Carroll, *Alice in Wonderland.*

Annuities aside, and that's a big aside since they are probably the biggest drawback to pensions, there are a few Foolish pension options you could explore. As long as a pension plan is not managed Wisely, it can have some merits. The tax breaks for a 40 per cent tax-payer are quite significant, after all. Fools, though, should not focus just on the tax efficiency of such schemes and as a result ignore the investment performance of the underlying fund.

The Government's promise of stakeholder pensions, which will not, by law, charge more than 1 per cent in fees annually, sounds very Foolish. The Wise have claimed they will be unable to offer such products, claiming they will only be able to invest in very basic funds such as ones which track the FTSE 100 index. Brilliant! That's superb, considering that nine-tenths of managed funds fail to beat this market average performance over the long run.

There are already some pension providers who offer such Foolish and flexible products. Most of them track the FTSE 100 or FTSE All Share Index. (The All Share incorporates approximately the largest 800 companies listed on the London stock exchange, whereas the FTSE 100 covers the top hundred.) The charges are 1 per cent or less per year and most are flexible, allowing people to either increase or even decrease their contributions, or take a break (or 'holiday') from contributions without fiscal penalty. Virgin Direct, for example, runs a simple scheme such as this.

Consider using such a flexible pension scheme as an insurance measure. Put in a certain amount each month, but, say, only a third of your total planned investments. This fund will build up and provide a basic income if you are unable to look after your own financial affairs in retirement, for health or any other unfortunate reasons. But don't wish all your savings away in such schemes in the hope that they will provide the best deal.

If you are feeling very Foolish and want to determine your own financial fate by selecting your own stocks and shares, something we will be encouraging you to consider over the next few chapters, then investigate another two acronyms: SIPPs and GPPs.

SIPPs stands for self-invested pension plans. These give the benefits of other pension schemes, such as tax breaks, but also the attendant drawbacks, such as forced annuity purchase. However, the main difference is that you choose the investments which make up the pension pot. In theory this sounds very flexible. You can invest in individual shares and cheap funds that track the index as well. However, such schemes are few and far between. Those which do exist are only offered by Wise finance providers who still charge exorbitant fees for 'looking after' your investments, and large dealing fees when you purchase or sell stocks or funds.

Another variant on this theme is the GPP, which stands for group pension plan. As the name suggests, these are flexible schemes organized by groups, whether they be employees of a small business, members of a sports club or a trade association. The group can choose which investments to back amongst themselves without Wise interference. And the charges of running such a scheme can be spread across the whole group, making fees much more economic.

Before moving on to Foolish alternatives beyond the pension scheme umbrella, pensions have one other advantage. If you feel you are impatient and might spend your savings before you retire, for whatever reason, keeping them locked up under a pension plan means you can't do this even if you are tempted to. Well you could, if you were prepared to incur immense fees for breaking the pension rules and requirements. For those with little willpower, this is quite an important point to bear in mind.

Fortunately, though, willpower is one attribute that is very Foolish, and it can be acquired without going through painful self-help courses involving walking over coals, or anything else (but there's a Foolish thought …). Over your investment life of forty years or more, you will experience many troughs and peaks. In order to feel the full Foolish effect of compounding rates of return, you will have to hold on during both extremes and resist the temptation to switch from your Foolish principles, despite the pleadings of the Wise.

Now, are you ready to discover some real financial Folly? Then step right this way …

To ISA or not to ISA?

PEPs, TESSAs, SIPPs, ISAs, BLIPs: why do the British love a tasty-sounding acronym? There's something terribly pleasing about a set of letters. But how many of us can really tell what they all mean? In this Motley collection you won't be surprised to hear that most stand for financial tools.

In the last section, we brought the lesser-spotted SIPP, or self-invested pension plan, out of its hiding hole. Admittedly, BLIP was there just to slip you up – no, it doesn't stand for British Life Insurance Plan, or even Bitter Losers and Idiots Party, in case you were wondering. The remaining three, PEPs, TESSAs and ISAs, are probably more familiar: all are tax-incentive schemes dreamt up by the Treasury over the past fifteen years to encourage people to save more money. As well as being in love with acronyms, inhabitants of the UK are also desperate to avoid paying tax if at all possible. The prospect of pissing off the Inland Revenue makes some people positively weak at the knees.

We've already seen how Wise pension providers have made full use of this weakness to tempt individuals to sock a blow at the taxman by taking out a pension policy. However, there are other ways of keeping the taxman at bay while keeping the interference of expensive and underperforming Wise men to a minimum. After all, the Wise are the real baddies in this whole financial scene, sucking you dry to the financial marrow. It is against them that the principal attack should be directed.

ISAs are one of the most effective ploys to use in your fight for financial felicity. These are merely the latest in a long line of Treasury toys designed to protect your lolly from any tax liabilities, principally the income or capital gains varieties. Like anything with a lengthy history, these instruments can be quite complicated, but I'm only going to go back one generation – to the ISA's immediate ancestors, Mr PEP and Ms TESSA. Before doing so, just bear in mind that all an ISA does is act as an outer casing, or shell, to protect your nest-egg from attack by predatory taxmen, eager to get their grubby hands on your lucre.

In the late 1980s the Chancellor of the Exchequer, then a certain grey-haired gentleman dubbed 'Nice' Mr Major, introduced investors to two schemes: the PEP, or Personal Equity Plan, and TESSA, or Tax-Exempt Special Savings Account. These were actually quite nice schemes. PEPs protected investments in equities (another name for stocks or shares) from capital gains or income tax. (Basically income tax is charged on the dividend payments a company pays you for holding its shares and capital gains tax comes from charging a rate on the difference between the price paid for a share and the price at which you sold the investment. The exact details are more complicated – you can find a fuller explanation later.) TESSAs did the same thing, giving tax protection for cash savings.

There were restrictions to both schemes. You could only shelter a certain amount of money each year in each scheme. TESSAs were far too sensible and, as befits their founder, conservative as well: you could only gain the tax-free benefits if you kept the money locked up for five years. This left the account holder at the mercy of the bank or building society running the account: if your provider cut interest rates on the TESSA, you could only either shrug and persevere with the lower rate in order to keep the tax breaks on any gains, or else forego them and try to find a better return. Returns were pretty paltry in any case, compared with those given by basic PEPs tracking the FTSE 100 index. Nevertheless, the idea to encourage long-term savings and investment was good and the scheme worked well in practice.

Switch to May 1997 and anything connected with that same 'Nice' Mr Major suddenly became tainted as 'New' Labour swept to power. Away with his monstrous PEPs and terrible TESSAs, swore 'Prudent' Mr Brown! In their place he has put the sparkly ISA, which merely stands for Individual Savings Account. But in effect this is merely a cosmetic attempt to combine both PEPs and TESSAs in one tax-efficient savings vehicle.

Unfortunately though, whereas the old system was simple because the different elements, cash or shares, were kept quite distinct in completely separate schemes, the replacement ISAs have become incredibly confusing. Because they combine all the various elements of the old scheme, the rules and conditions governing the whole ISA process are both complex and intimidating.

However, you'll be glad to know that with a little Foolish forethought, you won't need to fumble in the dark about all these ins and outs. No, all an ISA does is stop the taxman from grabbing his normal portion of your income or capital gains (which is the money, or gains, you have made from investing your capital, the original sum you started with). Think of an ISA as a wrapper keeping the Inland Revenue from your extra investment income and gains.

First, a few salient facts to remember about these remarkably Foolish financial weapons:

i) **At the time of writing (2000) you can only put a total of £5,000 into an ISA each tax year, beginning on 6 April.**

ii) **This can either go into a 'maxi' ISA or be distributed across up to three 'mini' ISAs.**

iii) **The three different types of mini ISA protect cash, life insurance and shares respectively from tax liabilities.**

iv) **You can only put a maximum of £1,000 into the first two types of mini ISA, but up to £3,000 into the shares-style mini ISA.**

v) In the maxi ISA, you can put all £5,000 towards investing in shares, free of tax, or else you can choose to put up to £1,000 in cash, another £1,000 in life insurance and the remainder in shares.

vi) Vitally, you can't take out a maxi ISA if you already have a mini ISA and vice versa.

There are other more technical details but we won't bother with them at the moment.

At the Fool we believe in long-term investment strategies. And over the long run, by which we mean most of this century, shares have outperformed all other investments. If you need further convincing, don't worry – we shall return to hammer this point home and display evidence for it later in this chapter!

ISAs should only be used for long-term financial planning, by which we mean at least ten years. This is because if you withdraw funds from the ISA much earlier in its lifetime, you won't be making the most you could from potential tax-free gains. Over longer periods of time, your gains should mount up progressively. You only have to pay capital gains tax when you realize, or sell, your investment, so you will benefit more by waiting for a longer period of time.

Therefore, because ISAs are best used as long-term investment vehicles and since shares perform the best over the long run, you should strongly consider using a maxi ISA to invest in shares alone, and ignore the other options. That would be the most Foolish thing to do.

Say, for example, you have £5,000 to invest over a year. If you put £1,000, the most you can, into a mini cash ISA, producing only a 7 per cent annual return at best, then you can only use £3,000 to pick shares, via a mini shares ISA, which return 11 per cent on average each year. That is £2,000 less than if you had used the full allowance of the £5,000 maxi ISA to invest in shares.

As for life insurance, forget it as an investment. If you have loved ones who would need supporting if you died suddenly, consider taking out a separate life policy to cover this sad eventuality, but don't confuse it with your life-long investment plans.

Look at this table, which compares the strategy of picking several mini ISAs with that of choosing just a maxi ISA over ten years:

	AFTER 2 YEARS	AFTER 5 YEARS	AFTER 10 YEARS
£1,000 cash in mini ISA growing at 7% p.a.	1,145	1,403	1,967
£3,000 shares in mini ISA growing at 11% p.a.	3,696	5,055	8,518
£1,000 life insurance in mini ISA, growing at 6% p.a.	1,124	1,338	1,791
Total from mini ISAs	**5,965**	**7,796**	**12,276**
£5,000 shares in maxi ISA growing at 11% p.a.	**6,161**	**8,425**	**14,197**
Difference in return (maxi minus minis)	196	629	1,921

Note what a dramatic and detrimental effect investing in mini cash ISAs can have on the total return from your savings. And since such instruments only let you salt away £1,000 a year, which amounts to less than £20 a week, you would do just as well to save that money in a conventional high interest and instant access savings account. That way you can put the money towards something else more rewarding quite easily and efficiently.

What you gonna do?
Now before we get carried away with the nitty-gritty, it's time to go back to that fundamentally Foolish precept: *you*. What me?

Yes you! We've been talking a lot about ISAs and their implications for everybody. However, in generalized discussions such as this, it's too easy to forget the particular financial focus of each individual. It's impossible to talk about ISAs in isolation. Everyone has completely different financial demands. It's up to you, and you alone, to decide what your particular ones are.

Hopefully, after reading and maybe acting upon the ideas in the first half of the book, you are now in a position to invest. But before actually putting your hard-earned cash behind some venture or other for the first time, consider what your objectives are. Ask yourself some questions to help you decide. Why do you want to save? How much will you need to realize your goal?

You may have many different plans and ideas. That's fine. Just remember to keep them all uppermost in your mind, above such fascinating details as the tax-efficiency of maxi ISAs over managed pension funds or other mind-numbing statistics. Such minutiae can obscure your overall masterplan. This is the trap the Wise want you to fall into, so you take out one of their highly charged but low-performing investment vehicles. Don't let the tax tail wag the investment dog. Keep your ideals and aims hung up before you on your way through the financial jungle. If you do this, although things might change in the short term, you won't get distracted from the path leading to your long-term goal.

And remember to have fun. Do what Walter Hagen, a famous American golf pro of the 1920s, recommended golfers to do whilst on their way round golf courses in top tournaments: 'Remind yourself you're only here for a short visit. So don't hurry. Don't worry. And be always sure to smell the flowers along the way.'

If over the eighteen holes of your investment life you remember this doctrine alone, you will probably do far better in your Foolish amateur way than many investment professionals who have been paid to perform.

Back to business ...

So bearing in mind the need to keep your investment ideals ahead of you, and before rushing into ISAs, remember you already do in fact have some tax breaks. Yes, that's right, the Government allows you to make £7,100 in capital gains each year without any questions or ISA protection. This amount will not be taxed.

£7,100 is quite a significant amount of money. It should be enough to contain most people's annual gains, as long as you are canny enough to juggle which gains or losses to realize in each tax year. Remember that if you make a loss on an investment it will reduce your total gains, perhaps bringing you back within the tax-free limit.

This £7,100 threshold is quite important, and something that many ISA providers will not reveal to you. There is no way to avoid paying income tax on the income you receive from interest payments or share dividend payments, unless you invest via an ISA. (Most large companies operating in established industries aim to pay dividends to shareholders. These are cash payments made from a company's profits.) But if you invest in a maxi shares ISA, as suggested above, most of your return will come as a result of the shares increasing in value rather than via any dividend payments. This is what is meant by a capital increase or gain.

Thus your returns from capital gains, if you decide to realize them, should be more substantial than any income you receive from dividends. So if each year you are already allowed to make £7,100 in capital gains before paying tax, then you may not think it worth your while to pay extra charges to an ISA provider to protect any further gains, because you would be hard pressed to realize any more!

Above, we showed how £5,000 invested in shares protected by a maxi ISA would grow at the rate of 11 per cent each year for ten years in all. After two years, a gain of only £1,161 on the original £5,000 capital sum would have been made. If realized at this time there would be no tax to pay on these gains, even if held outside the ISA, since the £7,100 limit would not have been reached. That is as long as we assume this is the only investment being made and realized at the time.

In fact it is only after nine years that the tax-free limit is breached for the first time. By that time a £7,790 gain will have been made, assuming steady annual growth of 11 per cent, on the initial £5,000 capital sum. This is £690 above the limit. However, the limit could well have gone up nine years hence, in line with inflation. If we decide to exercise this gain we will have to pay tax on just the surplus £690.

So using the average historic growth rate of leading shares, which is 11 per cent (actually, 12 per cent minus charges of 1 per cent), you will have to hold the ISA for at least nine years to gain any benefits of tax avoidance. Hang on beyond that and the tax-efficient wrapper becomes far more useful. Remember this is taking this ISA investment in isolation from any others you may have. This is why you should work out investing via ISAs in relation to your overall investment plans.

If you have been put off paying for an over-expensive pension plan which underperforms, consider using an ISA as an alternative means of building up your own pension fund. You could also use an ISA to build up significant sums of money over the long term (typically more than ten years) so that you can pay off your mortgage early, for example, or perhaps pay for your children's university education.

The thought of all that youth brings me on to young people. Official statistics from the Department of Social Security showed that in 1997, only 3 per cent of people aged between twenty and twenty-nine held PEPs (the predecessor of share-invested ISAs). In a sense, this is understandable, since ISAs don't hold much appeal if they are only worthwhile over ten years or more. However, as I have just said, if you are in your twenties you should compare them with the tax benefits of personal pension plans. Say you choose to invest in a cheap fund tracking the FTSE 100 index returning 12 per cent a year, what will be the best place to invest and shelter your £100 a month from tax – a pension plan or an ISA? Here are a few checkpoints to try to help you decide:

i) Remember you cannot put more than 17.5 per cent of your salary in a pension each year, until you reach the age of

thirty-five. With an ISA you are restricted to £5,000 a year. Only if you earned more than £28,500 a year would the ISA seem too restrictive compared with a pension, since £5,000 is approximately 17.5 per cent of £28,500.

ii) For every £100 saved from your net or 'take-home' salary in a pension fund, you receive the income tax back. A basic taxpayer will have paid almost £30 in tax. The Government will refund this, so your actual monthly investment into the pension fund will be £130. With an ISA the monthly sum will remain at £100.

iii) Fast-forward thirty years. Assuming an annual charge of 1 per cent, the average net return on both funds will have been 11 per cent per year. At this rate, the pension fund will have grown to £364,600 whilst the money protected by an ISA will be only £280,400.

iv) However, at least three-quarters of the accumulated pension pot must, under current rules, go to purchase an annuity. This gives an income which has to be taxed according to normal Inland Revenue rules. At current rates, this fund would give you an annuity paying, at best, roughly £30,000 a year gross, until you depart from the planet.

v) Looking at the ISA route, you can keep the majority invested. It's up to you whether you sell some of the units in your fund for cash, or to buy bonds or gilts which will produce an income. Either way the gains will be tax-free, as opposed to the income from the pension which is taxed. And don't forget the remaining fund will continue to grow.

So it seems it is a pretty even toss-up between the two schemes, depending on your own requirements and preferences. The forced annuity purchase is still the main drawback of the pension scheme. To get more details and discuss these tricky options with other Fools, the best thing might be to check recent discussions on the Motley Fool's *Pensions* message board.

Of course this scenario assumes that all the rules stay the same for the next thirty years. In practice, knowing the meddlesome practices of politicians, some of them are bound to change, most notably the tax brackets and rates. On the pension front, the annuity rules will hopefully be scrapped and the Government will allow its citizens and loyal tax-payers to use their hard-saved money as they please.

When introducing ISAs, the Government guaranteed their lifetime for at least ten years. One would hope so, since, as we have seen, it would hardly seem worth holding them for less than that. Even if they are scrapped, it seems likely that something equivalent will replace them. In any case, you will still be able to hold your existing ISAs – those with PEPs and TESSAs still hang on to those instruments.

What should you put in an ISA? Getting share aware …

As shown above, it seems that if you want to save quickly for a holiday or a car then ISAs may not be the best products for you. They seem best suited to long-term savings plans. In that case, what are the best investments to protect using this tax-efficient shelter?

You may often hear a colleague say 'I'm going to take out an ISA,' or a friend wonder whether one ISA is better than another. What do they mean? They are probably referring to professionally managed funds. These are heavily promoted by the Wise. People feel they are being clever in avoiding tax by 'buying an ISA'. But this lets the Wise disguise the performance of the particular fund they are flogging.

But we know how badly such managed funds actually perform. Let's roll out the bald facts again. Over the past five, ten and twenty-five years, less than 10 per cent of all the managed funds run by Wise and expensive professional managers have managed to match or better the FTSE 100 index.

For knock-out evidence to support this, go over to **www.index-tracking.co.uk**. On this site, WM, a consultancy company, has published a detailed study. This looked at the performance, over the past twenty years, of managed funds against funds that passively tracked the index. The study found that 'in any five-year annualized period, investors in an active [managed] fund had around a one in four chance of outperforming a tracker'. In other words, 75 per cent failed to match the index. Even more appalling was the finding that 'of the forty-six trusts with a twenty-year performance history, only four outperformed the index'. That means you would have to be lucky enough to select the 9 per cent of managed funds that beat the index. Otherwise, you would have done better just buying a tracker to do the work of beating 91 per cent of managed funds for you cheaply and simply.

Investors are beginning to take this message on board. An increasing amount of ISA providers are offering cheap and simple products which track either this index (the FTSE 100) or the All Share index, which tracks the performance of the shares in roughly the top 800 public companies in the country, as listed on the Stock Exchange. These funds charge fees of less than 1 per cent a year and no initial fee, as opposed to managed funds which charge as much as 5 per cent a year, for no noticeably better return.

In fact it should be possible to judge a fund by its charges. Don't bother buying one which charges over 1 per cent a year. Only index trackers can afford to charge less than this. Most incur fees of 0.5 per cent. This topic will be covered in more detail in the next chapter.

Before that, you might like to consider why investing in shares is such a good and Foolish thing to do with your money. You may be wondering what other homes for your cash there are and why they are not so Foolish. If so, cast your mind back to the first half of this book, when we looked at ways of scraping cash together to invest. There are two basic things you can do with your money. You can either spend it or save it. You can splash out on things like essential items and luxury goods. You can make other pleasurable purchases such as lengthy holidays, fast cars, tall yachts, dark chocolates, exotic vegetables, fine works of art and the rest of the goods at Selfridges.

But if you have any folding stuff left over, you're going to have to decide what to do with it. If you don't spend it on even more ephemeral goodies then, sensible Fool that you now are, you may decide to invest it. Think of investing as finding a home for the money that you have decided not to spend.

Now there are commonly thought to be three places to put your surplus cash. You can either keep it as cash, or as near to cash as possible; use it to buy bricks and mortar, or other property; or invest in some of the leading companies in the world, by purchasing shares in such enterprises.

There are many different ways of getting exposure to each of these methods of investment. If you wanted to keep the money as cash you could just stuff it under the mattress. But unless a sudden bout of deflation gripped the nation's economy making pure money more valuable, and this hasn't happened for over sixty years, the real purchasing power of this cash would decay. Alternatively you could, more conventionally, put the surplus money in a bank or building society account which would pay you interest at a certain rate.

How are these interest rates set? Well they all relate to the base rate set by Eddie George and his colleagues at the Bank of England. Few banks exceed this headline rate, which is in fact the rate at which the Government will lend money to them. Base rates partly relate to longer-term interest rates, which are applied to the Government's own borrowings via bonds of thirty years' length, issued by the Treasury (you can buy some at the Post Office).

These Government bonds, called gilts, are effectively IOUs given by the Government to the banks and individuals who buy them, promising to repay the money lent with interest at a certain annual rate. This influences interest rates throughout the monetary system, and dictates the return from keeping your money in a building society savings account. This allows individuals to compare the return from investing in this way against other methods. Since 1919, with average inflation rampant at 4 per cent, gilts have given only an average 6.1 per cent return each year, according to the Barclays Capital Gilt Equity Study. So, whilst everyone should have a certain amount of money for emergencies, keeping too much as cash is an idle waste. There are better returns to be had elsewhere in the investment arena.

OK that's cash, but what about the second option – investing in property? We've already covered this, in Chapter Four. If you own your own property, you should not think of this as an investment but a necessity. When calculating your net worth, leave your home out of the equation. We all have to live somewhere. And for most people this is an expensive thing to do. In order to buy a property the majority of Britons will have to take out a mortgage. So although this will have allowed you to buy your dream home, effectively you are tied by a ball and chain to your mortgage provider until you pay off the loan in full.

To get more exposure to the property area you can't just use your spare cash to buy another flat. Offering to buy your neighbour's garage probably won't pay off either. I doubt he's going to part with his spare bedroom or even his garden shed come to that. Property speculation and development is a risky rich man's game, since you are dealing in large lots – whole houses or flats. True, property prices have on average risen by 8.5 per cent since the end of the Second World War; but the thing we are talking about is your home, and you can't really liquidate where you live to realize such gains. And in any case we can find better returns than that.

This brings us on to the third major area for investment: that's right, shares, the pot of gold at the end of every Fool's rainbow. Shares are exactly what their name suggests. They give the owner a share in the business that originally issued these rights of ownership. So think of being a shareholder as being a part-owner of a business. As the business grows, makes more sales, takes a greater market share and returns a greater profit to its shareholders, sometimes in the form of dividends, so its rival companies consider it more valuable.

If someone wants to buy the business outright at this later stage, he has to spend more than before. Thus to become a part-owner is also more expensive. Those already holding an interest in the business will be reluctant to part with their share for less than their original outlay. Now, according to the Barclays Capital Gilt Equity Study, the value of shares in leading UK companies has, on average, increased by 12.2 per cent each year since 1919.

Investing in shares, or backing the performance of companies, is thus the most profitable form of investment over the long term. Also, it is almost as flexible as investing in cash – in some cases more so, since you can buy and sell shares more easily than bits of property and some Government bonds, for instance.

The only question now is how to go about picking particular companies to invest in, and how to do this cheaply in small and regular amounts. Step right this way for foolproof (or should this be Wise-proof!) and cheap methods of picking shares mechanically.

Self-select ISAs

Before we leave them, we need to have one last look at ISAs. Whilst we have generally been dismissive of Wisely managed ISA investment funds, we may have neglected to mention the self-select ISA. This can be quite Foolish, since you can wrap individual shares, chosen by your own Foolish self, in this tax-free wrapper.

Now before you leap at this opportunity, I'm afraid there are a few drawbacks. These can be costly and cumbersome in practice, provided as they are by the Wise. Because of this you might still be best off using your ISA allowance on a long-term index tracker. However, this vehicle might be worth considering when we discuss investing in individual shares in the next few chapters, particularly if you follow the Foolish strategy of holding shares for the long term and make few purchases during the year.

Savings plans and the impact of the Internet

Here at the Fool, as you may have gathered, we are rather keen on the Internet. Funny that. One of the best improvements the Internet has made to life generally is that it has brought down prices for myriad things. If you want a book, for example, you can order it very cheaply over the Internet.

And if you're not happy with the price of something at one place, you can easily check how much it is elsewhere by surfing for a few minutes on the Web. Offline retailers are going to be stuffed by their guarantees that they will match any cheaper price punters can find.

They were banking on the lethargy factor of shoppers not being able to tramp around all the stores in a particular district. With the Internet they can now do this all around the world!

If you want to put money in a savings account you will also benefit by being connected. The best rates for such savings vehicles are only available online. Yes, the Web is the place to find the highest interest rates nowadays. This is worth bearing in mind when you are saving cash for your first investment.

Ten Foolish things you can do rather than take out a pension:

1. Stakeholder pensions with low charges may be worth considering once they are launched.
2. Certain Self-Invested Personal Group Pensions and allow you to choose which investments to put into your pension. Beware of hidden charges.
3. Pensions are only useful if you feel you do not have enough willpower to lock your savings away until you retire.
4. ISAs allow you to shelter any gains or income you make from investments away from the taxman.
5. Don't be seduced by expensive Wise managed ISA funds. Consider a self-select or index-tracking ISA instead.
6. Cash and Insurance mini-ISAs aren't worth bothering with if you want serious long-term returns.
7. Only take out an ISA if you intend to hold on to the investments within it for more than five years.
8. Remember that you already have an annual capital gains tax allowance of £7,100.
9. Investing in ISAs over the long term, may prove a particularly Foolish way of saving for retirement. You don't have to pay tax on the proceeds of investments held within ISAs. However, you do on pension proceeds.
10. Over the long run blue chip shares have historically offered the best average annual returns for ISAs.

Chapter Seven – Be maniacally mechanical and meticulously methodical!

All the clever people said one thing, and all the fools said another. And by God, the damn fools were right!
Winston Churchill (Chancellor of the Exchequer in 1925 when sterling rejoined the gold standard, which proved to be a mistake.)

So we have decided that shares are the best instruments to invest in. Over the long term, equities, a general term for the shares of major UK companies, have outperformed all other available British investments. But how on earth, you might be wondering, should I choose which, out of the myriad opportunities I see stretched out in the newspaper pages devoted to listing such things, to back with my piddling amount of money? Tricky, particularly as you have over 2,500 options to choose from.

You think we've already made it trickier for you by ruling out investing through a professionally managed fund. There's no slinking off to use such lazy solutions! But remember this is for your own good, because over 90 per cent of them have failed to match the performance of the leading index of the top 100 shares in the UK over five, ten and twenty-five years. Such funds also charge individuals exorbitant amounts of money for the privilege of failing to match this market average.

Even if this compelling argument doesn't convince you, you will still have more than 2,000 different managed funds, in the form of unit or investment trusts, to choose from. That task might seem just as immense as picking individual shares. How can you tell which fund manager is going to be better than any of the rest? Will Mr X of Mighty Mega-fund pick better-performing shares than Ms Y of Wise Investments? How long will your phantom picker be doing his stuff for that particular fund in any case, before moving somewhere else for more money?

It's like the childhood party game of pinning the tail on a donkey. The grumpy donkey is always moving around. You, the private investor, are blindfolded, and not told about the hidden fees these funds charge. And in any case the fund is well and truly a donkey, unable in most cases to match the performance of the stock market, regardless of the carrots you place before it.

So, faced with this difficulty, you might as well try to choose the underlying shares themselves, rather than the wrappers strangling these investments. After all, there are only 2,500 shares of various different companies listed on the London stock exchange. And you can write off most of these. Over 1,500 are worth less than £30 million, too small and risky to bother looking at. Most of the remaining 1,000 shares are within the FTSE All Share. So, in effect, if you invest directly in shares, you will have fewer choices to make. The process will be cheaper than investing in a managed fund and you could easily outperform the returns of such so-called professionals.

If this still doesn't get you going and you'd prefer to lie back a little longer and find easier methods of investing, never fear. There are Foolish ways of catering for your tastes. Rather than picking shares yourself, you can easily beat 90 per cent of professional investors by getting a machine to pick a selection of them for you. Because this system is mechanized, involving next to no humans, it will also prove cheaper. Intrigued? Here comes the intricate part of the plan.

Buy the market and beat most money managers

As we keep saying, over 90 per cent of funds over the longer term of at least five years fail to match the performance of the market average. This average, or benchmark, is measured by the movement of either the index of the top 100 shares (the FTSE 100), or a similar index of the leading 800 shares (FTSE All Share). In that case, you might Foolishly think, why not buy these market indicators instead, if they're so infallible?

This is entirely possible and is in fact as easy as falling off a log. Over twenty different financial services companies now offer you the chance to beat their highly paid professional fund managers by simply buying a product that attempts to replicate the average performance of the market. On the BBC news bulletins each day, about the only financial figure that gets mentioned is the price of the FTSE 100. The newsreader intones, 'And in the City a short time ago the FTSE was up four points at 6,547 …' before moving on to a funny 'And Finally' story to gladden listeners' hearts. Soon, after buying a little piece of the FTSE, you will be more enthralled by the FTSE figure than the And Finally story (but we hope you don't fret on hearing the turbulent tosses and turns the market invariably takes!).

These financial products attempt to track the performance of the index both up and down, by mechanically buying and selling its constituents as they rise and fall. As a company leaves the index, it gets sold, and the incoming company replacing it gets bought. No qualitative decisions are made at all. The machine dumbly and meekly buys the necessary shares automatically. If someone had done this since the index was set up in 1984, they would have seen their original investment increase by more than six times. Not bad, eh, for an unthinking investment product.

Before the FTSE 100 was invented, most investors used the FTSE All Share index as a benchmark for the market. This tracks the performance of roughly the top 800 shares listed on the London stock exchange. Since this was formed in 1962, an initial investment of £100 would have grown to £3,160. Thus the average increase per year has been about 10 per cent. When looking at the performance of an investment, always compare it with the return you would have got from putting the same amount of money in the All Share index.

The great thing about index trackers is you can invest in them with very small amounts of money. Nearly all the many providers of such funds will allow you to invest as little as £50 a month. That works out at less than £2 per day – the price of a pint. So give up just one pint of beer a day and you can invest in a cheap fund which has, over a long period of time, risen inexorably by 12 per cent a year. Say you had put £50 a month, saved from giving up a pint of beer a day, into the FTSE All Share, starting in 1962 when the index was created and assuming today's prices. Today, thirty-seven years later, your savings would have grown to £410,000! Not bad at all.

Another advantage of such funds is that they are cheap. Since they are all trying to do the same thing, there is little to choose between them except price. Admittedly some index funds have less tracking error than others, which means they stay more closely aligned to the index. You might wonder how on earth a computer carrying out a series of programmed trades can fail to match the index at all. Well, some funds do not in fact track the whole index dogmatically. Instead, they include only a handful of some of the smaller companies, which make up less than 0.1 per cent of the whole index. This means if one of these neglected companies grows more quickly than average, the index provider will be behind the index slightly. But these errors are quite small and in the long run make little difference. Nevertheless, in the lower reaches of the wider All Share index of 800 companies, it is worth bearing tracking error in mind, since short cuts are more commonplace.

Tracking error aside, price, as I say, is the main thing separating different providers. You should be able to find a decent index tracker that has only a 0.5 per cent annual fee and no other charges, such as front-loaded initial fees (which are charged when contributions are first made).

One important point to check, before taking the plunge, is whether the particular provider you are considering will let you drip regular amounts of cash into the market. Don't worry, most will.

Even if you have a lump sum to invest, this method of feeding a little bit of your money into the market each month is the best way to invest regularly. This is because it takes the most vicious swings out of stock market investing. Everyone hears about the market when it crashes. These regular plunges probably put more people off buying shares than any other factor. The prospect of investing a hard-earned lump sum and then seeing the market spin downwards can be frightening. However, the market also lurches up from time to time. It's just that these leaps don't make good news for the media (but they do for investors, which means virtually everyone with savings nowadays). Over longer periods of time, these illogical movements balance out in favour of the rises. And, as we have shown before, the market has on average risen by 12 per cent each year since 1945.

The easiest way to match this steady 12 per cent annual rise is by putting a fixed amount of money into the market each month. Say you put in £100 a month starting in January. The index might stand at 6,000 at the beginning of the year. Let's say, then, that your £100 could buy sixty units of your particular index-tracking fund. During January the index tumbles 500 points. This means that at the beginning of February, your £100 will now be able to buy approximately sixty-five units. So you are buying more units when the market is low. Imagine that during February, the market rises 1,000 points. This will allow you to buy fifty-five units at the start of March. During March, say the index remains pretty steady and ends the month at 6,500. Over the quarter, it has gone up 500 points, or 8.3 per cent (a twelfth). This means that after three months you have invested £300, buying you 180 units in all. However, your return would be 8.8 per cent, because you bought more units at a cheaper price at the beginning of February. In total your £300 investment would now be worth £326.51.

If, instead, you had put in £300 at the beginning of the year, still buying you 180 units at the time, it would have become only £325. OK, after three months there is not a great deal of difference between the two sums (only £1.51 to be precise). However, if you follow this pattern over the course of several years, buying more units when the market is lower and less when the market is higher, then you should even out the worst veers and head-spinning turns of the market. This process is called pound-cost averaging. Ask about it if you buy an ISA.

The essential point is that if you have a largish sum to invest, say anything over £1,000, you don't have to risk it all in one go, only to see the index plummet the day after you have bought your tracker. No, rather than risk that inheritance left by your beloved Great Aunt Nora, you can hang back and drip it in steadily in £100 lumps over a series of months. Then if the crash comes the next day, you will only see a tenth of your money fall. The next tenth can be used to pick up the index at this much lower point, giving you more units for the same amount of cash. And so on for thirty-seven years, or until Auntie's money has gone … How Foolish is that?!

Apart from the availability of pound-cost averaging, there are a couple of other things to check before buying an index tracker. Check if you can protect your contributions from tax by sheltering your investment in an ISA. This will help if you want to hold the index for a long time (which we hope you Foolishly will), as it will stop you from becoming liable to capital gains and income tax later on.

Then you have to decide which index to track. In the UK, the commonest available options are the FTSE 100 or All Share indices. The FTSE 100 covers the top 100 companies in the country by market size. The All Share tracks the largest 800 companies listed on the London stock exchange. There is not as much difference between them as the names suggest. In fact, because the FTSE 100 contains so many large companies it accounts for over 80 per cent of the All Share. The All Share, however, contains smaller companies that might rise exponentially and faster than many FTSE 100 companies, which might attract you to this option. Remember, though, that the FTSE 100 will pick up these companies eventually, as they grow.

You can also buy overseas indices such as the American S&P 500 index, which tracks the top 500 US shares. However, many of these index funds cost quite a bit more than their UK equivalents. They shouldn't do, but unfortunately their charges are generally higher at the moment. This might put you off such diversification. Also, data for countries beyond Europe, the US and Australia is less reliable, as such countries have less developed equity, or stock, markets. This means that returns from index tracking have not been quantified to the same degree.

For the latest information about the best trackers, please look at the *Index Trackers* message board on the Motley Fool Web site. This is where debates about fees, tracking error and regular payments are conducted. If you have any queries, why not pose a question? Regular contributors will be more than happy to answer it.

All investors, whether they have a lot or a little to invest, should use such index trackers as the secure foundation for their lifetime investment portfolio holdings. To return to the gardening metaphor employed at the front of the book, think of index trackers as laying a portion of your garden down to grass. This lawn will always look well-tended, and after a while will seem easy to care for. Some years' growth will be great, and you will reap rich returns as you mow. In other seasons the cuttings will be leaner. Never mind, because over a long period of time the returns will average out to give roughly the same each year. By drip feeding a little cash into this index tracker over a long period of time you will smoothly manage to match this accumulated return.

And remember the power of compounding such regular rates of return. £100 invested each month, growing at 12 per cent on average per year, will grow to £99,000 after twenty years, £350,000 after thirty years and an amazing £1,176,000 after forty years. That's the sort of thoughtless and Foolish investment we're after!

Spend fifteen minutes a year and Beat The Footsie

If investing in an index-tracking fund is like laying down a lawn in your garden – painless and pretty effective – then other mechanical share-picking strategies, which require slightly more care and maintenance, resemble tending herbaceous borders. Plants placed in such beds need to be chosen carefully so that they fit into a harmonious whole. Once planted, then each year they must be pruned into shape and maintained. But apart from a little care like this, such hardy plants can survive quite happily on their own.

At the Motley Fool we have devoted a whole section of our Web site to this style of investing, and have called it the *Foolish Workshop*. This is because such investments require a little work each year – in fact about fifteen minutes. Then they can be left alone until the same time next year. Let me explain these ramblings.

Above we explained how, by passively following the performance of the market average index, you can beat the returns of 90 per cent of professional money managers. Still, after completing this satisfying and painless task, you may think the average is not enough for you and your out-of-the-ordinary attributes. If the average is better than 90 per cent of money managers, then some people must do better than the market average. Are there any ways of picking shares mechanically to join the higher echelons?

Well, you'll be glad to hear that there are indeed some Foolproof methods you might like to follow. The Internet contains a vast amount of information. Fools have suggested various mechanical share-picking methods and several have been tried and tested electronically, making use of this wealth of data.

The most popular and widely followed is called Beating The Footsie or BTF for short. As the name suggests, the aim of the process is to beat the annual performance of the FTSE 100. This involves picking five shares each year from an old-style index called the FT 30. This is based on the style of America's Dow Jones Industrial Average, which also contains thirty companies. A committee picks thirty public companies, broadly representing the various industries that make up the economy. Unlike the FTSE 100 companies, which are selected purely by how large they are, size does not matter for the FT 30. The current thirty members of this index, at the beginning of 2000, are:

Allied Domecq
BG
Blue Circle Industries
BOC Group
Boots
BP Amoco
British Airways
British Aerospace
British Telecom
Cadbury Schweppes
Diageo
EMI Group
GKN
Glaxo Wellcome
Granada
ICI
Invensys
Lloyds TSB
Marconi
Marks & Spencer
National Westminster Bank
P & O Steam Navigation
Prudential Corporation
Reuters
Royal & Sun Alliance
Scottish Power
SmithKline Beecham
Tate & Lyle
Tesco
Vodafone Airtouch

This list can be found at the FTSE Web site (**www.ft-se.co.uk**) or by telephoning 020 7448 1810. Notice that most companies are also members of the FTSE 100, except Tate & Lyle. Now, from this list, how do you select the magic five that have tended to beat the performance of the FTSE 100 over the past fifty years or so? Well, as you would imagine, we are looking to find those most likely to rise in value over the coming year.

Remember these are all leading companies, unlikely to go bust. This would suggest that the shares most likely to rise over the year are those which currently seem out of favour. This is because investors will eventually see that they are undervalued, or cheap, and then begin to purchase them. So followers of the BTF strategy are looking for the five cheapest shares each year, in the belief that they will rise over the coming year. One way to tell that a share is cheap is to look at its dividend yield. Now I know that to bring up such delicate techniques of valuation, before talking about how to pick individual shares, is slightly running ahead of things. However, it's time for a little lesson in dividend yields.

Divide the last annual dividend payment by the current share price and you will have the dividend yield. Times it by one hundred to present it as a percentage. Thus if Bloggs Bathmakers plc paid out total dividends of 10p last year, and its shares currently trade at 200p, then Bloggs' dividend yield is currently 5 per cent (10/200 x 100 = 5).

Now if you bought these shares at 200p, you would hope Bloggs would pay out a dividend of at least 10p again next year. Unless profits were really affected because rival bathmakers had pulled the plug on Bloggs' market, this would be the case. Large companies in the FT 30 rarely cut dividends. If they did, this would make the company very unpopular and give shareholders little confidence in the group's long-term strategy. Indeed, many might sell their shares.

A 5 per cent return in the form of dividend payments is not bad, considering that if you put the same money in a bank savings account you would get a return of 6 per cent at most at the time of writing. To return to the FT 30 strategy, list the shares with the ten highest dividend yields. These are the ones that have lower share prices than usual. Over the coming year, you would expect these shares to rise the most – they are currently the 'cheapest' since they offer the best value dividend yield. Even if they do not, at least you should receive a decent dividend payment. At the time of writing these ten shares are:

Royal & Sun Alliance
Marks & Spencer
ICI
Allied Domecq
British Airways
Scottish Power
Blue Circle Industries
Tate & Lyle
Boots
BP Amoco

The BTF model takes the five lowest share prices from amongst these top ten. This is because psychologically people believe these shares are cheaper, even though they're not necessarily. This strategy has been comprehensively back-tested, so I suppose it has been shown to work more effectively than merely picking the shares with the top five highest yields. Certainly this has worked in the Dogs of the Dow strategy for American shares.

However, in the UK, the *Foolish Workshop* has discovered that the five highest-yielding shares in the top ten of the FT 30 actually provide just as good a return as the lowest-priced. So we recommend ignoring the American plan of picking the five lowest-priced of the top ten, and just picking the top five highest-yielding shares in the FT 30, full stop.

Then, after selecting this Foolish five and buying them cheaply through an execution-only broker (see box in the next chapter), in proportionate amounts (using a fifth of your cash for each one), most importantly do nothing for a whole year. That's your fifteen minutes up! Collect all the dividends, and remember to keep a note of the total amount you received from the various companies, since this is going to be reinvested in the scheme. Then a year later go through the whole process of selecting the next Foolish five.

Remember the FT 30 can change at random moments, so get a fresh list. Sell last year's shares and buy the five new ones (unless of course some remain the same). Again, you must buy them in proportionate amounts so that each company works out as a fifth of your portfolio initially. A helpful shortcut is to look in the *Foolish Workshop* section of the Motley Fool Web site, where the current Foolish five are already selected: **www.fool.co.uk/workshop/ workshoprankings.htm**.

Over the past sixteen years, as mentioned above, this BTF method has been tested. It has shown a 25 per cent annual return over sixteen years, comprehensively beating the FTSE 100 index at 12 per cent per year. Over one year the BTF method may not work. In other years it might work spectacularly well. But over the long run, and this is a long-term strategy, the BTF will show significant returns. If you do decide to follow this mechanical method, the best thing is to stick to it rigidly. It should come good eventually.

Now hang around, you might say. This is all very well – I might be a Fool, but I'm not stupid. I can't just drip in a small amount of money each month, as I can with an index tracker, because I've got to buy five whole equal-sized chunks of shares. That's going to cost a bit, what with all the brokerage charges as well. Aha, you've seen the flaw for fiscally challenged investors in Beating The FTSE.

True, because of the charges, BTF is probably most effective if you have about £5,000 to invest so that you can put £1,000 in each of the Foolish five. Any less and your returns might be eaten away by the excessive fees charged by brokers when you buy the shares. At present the broker with the best deal will still charge you a minimum of £10 per trade. With 0.5 per cent stamp tax included as well, the total charges on a purchase of £1,000 worth of shares will be 1.5 per cent (£15 in all). Buy in smaller amounts and you will be charged proportionately more on the transaction. The shares will have to perform better to overcome this initial charge.

So if you are keen on this particular method you will first have to build up sufficient funds in a savings account. Consider a high-interest instant access online one, like Egg's at **www.egg.com**. You can contribute to this by direct debit. This is a good habit for all investors to get into. If you save only £200 per month, you will have enough to invest in the BTF within two years.

You'll be glad to know, though, that there are shortcuts available. Perhaps the BTF Lite is the best one in this situation.

Again, this involves sorting the FT 30 according to dividend yield, then taking the top ten highest yielding shares, as with the full scale BTF strategy. But rather than taking the five shares with the lowest, or 'cheapest' share prices, choose just the two lowest. Buy these two shares, spending £1,000 on each. Hold them for a year. Sell them. Select the next two shares from the FT 30 using this method, buy them, and repeat the process until you've made enough to retire or set off on your travels!

This method has been back-tested since 1983 using historic data. Although more volatile than picking the full Foolish Five each year, the BTF Lite has given a better return than the normal BTF: 29.3 per cent compared to 25 per cent. The standard deviation from the average in each year was 24.2 per cent, compared with 22 per cent for the normal BTF.

As any Fool knows, nobody can predict what is going to happen in the markets in the future, but these mechanical methods have shown that over quite long periods of time, unemotional stock-picking strategies have invariably worked better than many individual and idiosyncratic methods. There are many other ways of constructing such schemes and testing them, many of them similarly based around selecting high dividend-yielding shares. Several of these ideas are discussed in more detail in the *Foolish Workshop* area of the Motley Fool Web site and the various message boards linked to each strategy.

Before moving on to the more artistic policy of selecting your own shares, you might like to consider why scientific strategies like Beating The Footsie work. Well, many academics would have us believe that the stock market can be explained rationally. Such boffins claim that the market should in theory be efficient, with all the news and figures already priced into various shares. People or funds who own the shares are all meant to have rational reasons for doing so.

However, in practice, this robotic efficiency doesn't exist. Human sentiment, of course, plays a large part in the reasons why some shares are more popular than others. In short, some stocks are pushed up artificially high, beyond what scientists believe to be their real value, whilst other shares are marked down viciously when in reality the company's financial performance has only slipped up slightly.

Mechanical strategies, such as the BTF, thrive on this so-called inefficiency. By picking, like a robot, those shares which will recover and thrive but have temporarily fallen, a portfolio can outperform in the long run. So the theory goes. However, if you still hanker after playing your own unique role in this investment process, then let's try and find out how to pick shares cheaply and decide upon a decent way of doing this for the long term.

Foolish health warning before attempting to Beat The Footsie

Beating The Footsie, by its mechanical nature, requires a particularly stern mind-set. Remember you are buying companies that are temporarily out of favour with the general investment community. Taking this contrary approach can be good, because the general investment herd tends to take on a short-term Wise appearance. Private investors can get sucked into this frenzy just before such fashionable shares crash.

However, lurking on the edge of this excitement can be tough. These unloved BTF shares may well go down over the year you hold them. You will then have to be very strong to follow the same strategy the next year. If your supposedly undervalued shares underperform the market again the next year, you will have to have an extremely focused and blinkered approach to continue with the BTF strategy. You might think it is a long-term terminal decline rather than a temporary blip.

But this disciplined approach must be followed if the strategy is to work and beat the Footsie over the long term. The following year, the shares could rise 50 per cent, beating the Footsie handsomely and showing an overall market-beating return. Only then, after three years, will the strategy have 'worked'.

If you don't think you could stand this relatively short-term worry, then perhaps index tracking is more suitable. Many people don't have the patience to hold out that long. That's partly why the BTF works – because it is an approach that is contrary to the one most people follow, and deliberately picks temporarily unloved shares.

You will have to have a certain amount of patience to hold on to a fund tracking the index, too, because that will only really prosper over the long run, say five or ten years minimum. However, through pound-cost averaging schemes, at least you can steadily drip small amounts into the market on a regular basis, avoiding the worst peaks and troughs. With Beating The Footsie you are more exposed, since you have to buy £5,000 worth of shares to follow the strategy.

Alternatively, there are other Foolish mechanical strategies, which might be worth exploring and may prove more suitable for your particular mind-set. Take a look at the Workshop *section of the Motley Fool Web site for more details.*

Five Foolish methods of investing mechanically:

1. If you still don't want to wade through the more than 800 shares in the FTSE All-Share Index to choose several to invest in, employ a machine to mechanically select shares.

2. Buy the market and beat most money managers. Funds tracking the performance of either the FTSE 100 or All-Share indices should be the basis of many Fools' investments. This has returned 12 per cent on average each year since 1919.

3. Pound-cost averaging, which involves dripping small amounts monthly into such funds, will allow you to avoid the worst peaks and troughs of the index.

4. Spend fifteen minutes a year and Beat the Footsie. This involves picking once a year the five 'cheapest' shares from the FT30, ranked by dividend yield. Over the past sixteen years this has shown an average 25 per cent annual return. Since you should invest in sums of £1,000 per share, consider looking at the BTF Lite method, which involves picking only the two cheapest shares each year.

5. You have to have a contrary nature to Beat the Footsie. It involves picking out-of-favour shares, which may fall. You may only see returns after several years of losses.

Chapter Eight – The jewel in the Foolish investment crown: buying a part of individual companies

> ...now thou hast avenged
> Supplanted Adam, and, by vanquishing
> Temptation, hast regained lost Paradise...
> John Milton, *Paradise Regained*

Congratulations, Fool, on making it this far through the investment jungle. No doubt along your way you have had to slash away many poisonous Wise vipers hanging down from the trees, avoid the high-spending traps left open on the forest floor and clear the debt laid down in your path.

If you have not been tempted by other methods of gaining financial glory then here, in this clearing, lies the holy grail – the inner sanctum of investment, where we shall unveil the gems that will take you through your investment life happily. Then at last you can rest from your weary labours and reap the rewards of your valiant trip.

The company investment arena has rarely looked as promising and inviting for individual investors as it does now. The information age has opened up a mass of corporate knowledge that previously lay buried in vaults open only to the Wise. This material now lies open to all in its full electronic glory, stored on Internet servers and thus available on the World Wide Web. At the same time, the charges incurred from dealing in shares have progressively fallen. Nowadays discount brokers, who execute trades for individuals without giving advice, offer deals charging on average 1 per cent commission, and in many cases less, especially on introductory offers. In the past, dealing by telephone was the only way to perform this necessary part of the investment process. Now this can be done even more cheaply over the Internet.

Choosing a broker

Up until recently, if you wanted to invest directly in the stock market by buying individual shares you had to use a very expensive person called a broker. He would give you advice about which companies to buy, charge extortionate amounts for the privilege, and would not even take you on unless you could stump up a rather large amount of money before dealing.

Roughly twenty years ago, in the early 1980s, a whole host of individual investors came on to the scene. This was due to the Government's massive privatization programme, which saw nationalized companies, like BT and British Gas amongst others, float on the stock exchange and offer the general public shares.

Following this upsurge in interest, high street banks and other similar operators offered a service in selling these shares in privatized companies simply and cheaply, and in buying other companies' shares at the same time. These share shops executed the buy or sell order only. The brokers running them did not offer any Wise advice about whether this was a good or bad time to do it. Thus the costs were much cheaper.

Advisory brokers make their money by commission; therefore, they encourage their clients to trade as much as possible to generate extra commission. So the brokers that only execute orders without giving advice are far preferable, because they do not encourage clients to waste their money on charges generated via extra unnecessary trades.

From this route sprang all manner of execution-only, or discount, brokers. You can now choose from over twenty in the UK. The Motley Fool Web site lists all the various deals that they offer. The choice can be quite bewildering.

Here, then, are a few things to consider when choosing a broker to execute your share-buying decisions. For a full overview, look at this section of the Motley Fool Web site: **www.fool.co.uk/PersonalFinance/ DiscountBrokers/DiscountBrokers1.htm**.

The first thing to look at is whether you want to use the telephone or Internet to execute your trading decisions. At present, many brokers are encouraging people to set up Internet accounts by making introductory offers, since this is cheaper for their administration. Some of the cheapest brokers, such as the Share Centre, only deal at certain times of day to keep costs to a minimum as well. This should be OK if you plan to hold the shares for a long period of time. You will not notice daily discrepancies after a few months.

Basically, choosing a broker is like choosing a mobile telephone. Those with lower introductory charges may not necessarily be best in the long run. Their service may not prove to be as good, since they may become engulfed with customers opening accounts. On the other hand, commission should be kept to a minimum – you don't want to give the Wise too much for merely transferring shares between clients!

There are two other things you should decide at the outset. One is whether you want to receive share certificates and be registered as a shareholder with the company. This costs more nowadays, because basically, to cut their costs, many brokers buy a whole block of shares and their clients own a slice of it via this pooled 'nominee' account. If you own the shares directly, you will get annual reports and be able to attend and vote at AGMs. This last option, whilst being more expensive, can prove Foolish.

The other thing to consider is whether your broker will reinvest any dividends you receive from your shareholdings to buy further shares in the company. This is extremely Foolish, since this is the way to boost your returns, via the miracle of compounding. Unfortunately many brokers charge for this service. For more information on Dividend Reinvestment Programmes see the section later in this chapter.

Finally, you may wish to buy shares in companies listed on stock exchanges other than London's. For example, Microsoft is listed on Nasdaq, the American technology-based exchange. If you want to do this, you should inquire if this is possible before opening your brokerage account.

These technological leaps forward have enabled individual private investors to regain control of their finances electronically, free of suspect professional advisers. But having thrown off these barriers to entry, you will still be faced with the age-old dilemma of where to put your surplus cash. Which investments should you back?

Before rushing headlong into the latest hot thing, remember that even though the technology has changed, providing you with an easier means of access, solid financial principles have not. It might be easier to day trade, but that still doesn't make this particular form of gambling any more profitable than shoving your cash on the horses.

No, unfortunately there is no magic formula for finding fabulous investments. It is at this stage, before committing funds to particular companies, that you should consider your whole financial outlook. Again ask yourself what your particular aims are. Why do you want to invest? What do you want to achieve? What time-frame have you got to achieve these investment goals?

Each individual will have different plans. However, above all, remember that investment takes time. Speculations can be over in a matter of moments. The flutter of a heartbeat can divide the winner from the fallers at the first fence. Investment will continue for a lifetime, though, and deciding where to place your money to get the safest, surest and yet still sufficient return involves a continual learning process.

With this in mind, it is worth studying the strategies of successful investors, like Warren Buffet, the Sage of Omaha. This investment legend has achieved consistent returns of above 25 per cent a year over the last thirty years or more. Surely that success is worth following in greater detail? Another successful investor whose ideas are worth looking at is Peter Lynch. From 1977 to 1990, he managed the flagship Magellan fund for American investment company Fidelity Management, producing an average annual return of 29 per cent during that period. Funnily enough, although we abhor most Wise-managed funds, it's worth taking a peek at Lynch's style, which is surprisingly Foolish. Both Buffet and Lynch have either written books about their methods or had books written about them.

Test your own ideas and strategies by setting up a paper portfolio. This can be done on the Motley Fool Web site. You can follow what would have happened to your proposed investments, based on your decisions. This is a useful and painless way of finding out whether your investment ideas are any good. Perhaps the best way of improving your chances is educating yourself about basic investment techniques and common Foolish sense whilst you are saving money for your first investments.

If you decide that you do not trust your own investment ability, then that's fine and you can follow some of the mechanical strategies outlined in the last chapter. This is why everyone should invest in an index tracker before branching out to test their own theories.

Good, having set out today's investment scene and encouraged individuals to sort out their own particular investment plans and goals, I think it's time to drag the first Foolish investment principle on to the stage.

Research the future

Now don't be put off by the connotations of the word 'research'. We're not asking for in-depth studies into particular companies, why they are going to take over the world and how they're going to achieve this objective. Just be certain that if you decide to buy shares in a particular company, you can really satisfy yourself that your reasons for buying are sound. In order to do this, you will need to do a little research. If you cannot do this, and only believe the shares are worth buying because someone recommended them to you or because you like some of the company's products, that is not sufficient.

Investment should not be undertaken lightly. Let's look at

master investor Warren Buffet again. He has said that investors should consider their investment life as a blank piece of card. Each time you decide to invest, you should punch a hole in the card to represent that investment. If you decide to invest in another company, you have to punch another hole in the card. Now the card will only take a certain number of holes. Buffet suggests less than twenty punch holes throughout your lifetime.

So be certain when you decide upon an investment that it has at least a reasonable chance of lasting a lifetime. There is nothing to stop you from topping up that investment when you have more funds, but you should only change your investment and sell it if you become convinced that something fundamental about the company and its future potential profitability has changed. Buffet has held some of the stocks in his portfolio, like Coca-Cola, for over twenty years, steadily increasing his holding in the company.

However, as we have said, there are currently about 1,500 companies in the UK worth more than £30 million and therefore candidates for an investment portfolio. That means, if we are going to make do with a maximum of twenty investments in all, that only one in every seventy-five will do for your portfolio. So there are plenty of fish in the investment sea. Do not feel rushed into making an investment. There are many paths you can go down, explore and assess before placing your precious money.

Now if we are looking for investments to last a lifetime, we should not be looking at them from the perspective of the present, or the immediate future. No, no. Instead project yourself forward to the end of your planned investment period. If you are thirty and want to start drawing on your investments when you reach the grand old age of fifty-five, put yourself in the position of someone twenty-five years hence, in 2025. Even then, you can still expect to hold some of these shares for perhaps another twenty years.

Who knows exactly what the world will be like at that point? Aliens might well have invaded the planet. So perhaps we should prepare for this fate and watch *First Contact* again. This invasion could have disastrous consequences for world civilization.

People's portfolios could well and truly become defunct as investments like Cyberzmurgys in Intergalactic Travel (whatever they are) replace shares in global companies as the choice investment for our alien cousins.

In the unlikely event that this takes place, there's not much you can do wherever you place your money. However, we'll have to assume that no external forces are going to come along to unbalance our world picture within the next twenty-five years. Before we start crystal ball-gazing, though, it might be useful to look at today's leading twenty-five companies and work out what they were up to twenty-five years ago, in 1975.

In terms of market value, here are the top twenty-five companies listed on the London stock exchange at the beginning of 2000:

COMPANY	VALUE (BILLIONS)	SECTOR	AVERAGE ANNUAL RETURN IN 1990s	
BP Amoco	£121.3	Oil	47.2%	11th
BT	£98.4	Telecom	85.6%	3rd
Vodafone AirTouch	£95.4	Telecom	129.1%	1st
HSBC	£73.0	Financial	n/a	
Glaxo Wellcome	£63.7	Pharmaceutical	55.4%	10th
Shell T&T	£51.2	Oil	39.4%	12th
Astra Zeneca	£45.6	Pharmaceutical	n/a	
SmithKline Beecham	£44.4	Pharmaceutical	58.2%	8th
Lloyds TSB	£42.4	Financial	94.6%	2nd
GEC / Marconi	£29.8	Electronic/Telecom	85.5%	4th
Barclays	£26.6	Financial	59.4%	7th
Cable & Wireless	£25.5	Telecom	38.3%	13th
Orange	£25.0	Telecom	n/a	
Prudential	£23.8	Financial	73.4%	6th
NatWest	£22.2	Financial	56.1%	9th

Colt Telecom	£21.2	Telecom	n/a	
BSkyB	£17.2	Media	n/a	
Diageo	£17.0	Beverages	10.2%	18th
Anglo American	£16.8	Mining	n/a	
Rio Tinto	£15.9	Mining	28.5%	16th
Halifax	£15.4	Financial	n/a	
Abbey National	£14.1	Financial	75.4%	5th
BG	£14.0	Gas	34.0%	14th
Unilever	£13.3	Food Producer	27.2%	17th
Tesco	£12.8	Retail	31.6%	15th

(By the way, the best-performing shares during the 1990s were in accountancy software developer Sage. The company grew in value by on average 314.1 per cent each year during the decade. If you had invested £1000 in Sage on 1 January 1990, by 31 December 1999 that small sum would have grown to a remarkable £315,070!)

In 1975 almost half of these companies were not public. In other words, you would not have been able to buy shares in them. BT and BG (the old British Gas) were both nationalized industries, owned and run by the Government. They were only privatized in the 1980s. Although the four main high street banks (HSBC, Lloyds TSB, Barclays and NatWest) were in existence, the Halifax and Abbey National were both mutual building societies, owned by their members. You could have invested in the Prudential though.

The three large pharmaceutical companies (Glaxo Wellcome, SmithKline Beecham and Astra Zeneca) were around, but not in exactly the same state as these modern merged entities. Similarly Diageo existed as Guinness and Grand Metropolitan independently. Food producer Unilever, also maker of household goods like Persil washing powder, was thriving, as was the long-lived electronics group GEC and the oil group Shell.

Top supermarket chain Tesco has only really become dominant in the past few years. In 1975 it was a much smaller operation. Mining behemoths Rio Tinto and South African group Anglo American (part owner of De Beers diamonds) were around, though Anglo American was listed on the Johannesburg stock exchange.

The real surprise has been the telecom sector, with cabling companies Cable & Wireless and Colt Telecom growing exponentially. Most amazing of all, mobile phone developers Vodafone and Orange were only founded in the 1980s, and Orange has only really taken off in the past few years. Satellite television broadcaster BSkyB also emerged to prominence in the early 1990s.

Now let's see which companies were in fact the largest, by market value, in 1975:

COMPANY	VALUE	SECTOR	(VALUE IN 2000)
British Petroleum	£1,313m	Oil & Gas	(£121,300m)
Shell T&T	£1,221m	Oil & Gas	£51,200m
ICI	£999m	Chemicals	(£4,900m)
British American Tobacco (BAT)	£684m	Tobacco	(£7,200m)
Unilever	£570m	Food	£13,300m
Marks & Spencer	£569m	Retail	£8,840m
General Electric (Marconi)	£540m	Electrical	£24,850m
Barclays	£374m	Bank	£26,600m
Commercial Union (CGU)	£399m	Insurance	(£12,000m)
Great Universal Stores (GUS)	£391m	Retail	£4,160m
Imperial (Tobacco)	£374m	Tobacco	£2,940m
Distillers (Diageo)	£363m	Beverages	(£19,320m)
National Westminster Bank	£337m	Bank	£22,200m
Boots	£310m	Retail	£5,750m
Rio Tinto Zinc	£300m	Mining	£15,900m

Royal Insurance (Royal & Sun)	£279m	Insurance	(£6,575m)
Beecham (SmithKline)	£274m	Pharmaceutical	(£44,400m)
Allied Breweries (Diageo)	£261m	Brewing	(£19,320m)
Midland Bank (HSBC)	£251m	Bank	(£73,000m)
Glaxo (Wellcome)	£251m	Pharmaceutical	(£63,700m)
Courtaulds	£245m	Textiles	£83m
Land Securities	£238m	Property	£3,860m
Rank Organization	£233m	Entertainment	£1,560m
Prudential Assurance	£227m	Assurance	£23,800m
Lloyds Bank	£227m	Bank	(£42,400m)

(Figures in brackets: you cannot strictly compare the values of these companies in 1975 with their successors today. The number of changes in the share capital of the companies, such as mergers, makes it impossible.)

Although the benefit of hindsight is immense, it would have been quite possible to make several sensible decisions in 1975 as to what types of companies would have survived the succeeding twenty-five years. Banks are great survivors in any market economy, as they provide money for other businesses and enterprises. Everybody uses the products of drug makers and developers. Oil, gas and other mineral producers provide the necessary fuel to keep the country going. And food, drinks and household goods makers and retailers are necessary to keep everyone fed, clothed and washed. All these companies have made significant and consistent profits over this period. In the same time, their shares have increased massively in value as well.

To predict the emergence of telecom players would have required real foresight. American investors would have had an even more surprising twenty-five years, with the emergence of computer-related companies such as software producer Microsoft and silicon chip maker Intel. Apart from telecom players, Tesco would have proved a very shrewd investment for someone who recognized the virtues of clever management and cheap prices at a time when supermarkets were rapidly replacing traditional grocers.

Can you see how these companies are dividing into two separate groups? They are not completely exclusive of each other, but there is certainly a difference between them. In the first group are companies that remain consistently at the top of the pile, and are inventive enough to hold their position easily against all comers. These tenacious survivors would include the companies on the top twenty-five list in both 1975 and 2000: the high street banks; leading oil and mining companies; food and drinks producers; and some drug concerns. To last twenty-five years at the top of the pile and still remain the leader of their respective sectors requires some skill. Many rivals are attempting to knock these top companies off their perches.

Such dominant companies are in danger of becoming complacent, though. This has happened recently at the nation's one-time favourite high street retailer, Marks and Spencer. The group became used to thinking that soaring sales were easy to achieve, and failed to notice a change in the seemingly trifling matter of shoppers' attitudes, which is in fact vital. In a similar fashion, Tesco has replaced J Sainsbury by market share as the top grocer in the country, and has accordingly been given favoured status by the stock market.

This first type of company may not grow much in terms of raw product sales, having reached saturation point in its particular market, or at least its domestic one (that is, of course, after stripping out the effects of inflation on these sales figures). Investors in these companies may instead be looking for consistent profits and hence dividend payments.

This, remember, is how the Beating The Footsie strategy works – by selecting solid companies that are temporarily out of favour with investors, which therefore produce the most generous dividends per share. The business might become more efficient and could expand overseas or into new markets, possibly by acquiring other businesses. It should follow both strategies to create more profits. But essentially there is not a great deal of growth to come from these businesses.

The second type of company are those which were nowhere to be seen in the 1975 list of top dogs, but which have since emerged to prominence in dramatic fashion. In this second category you would include the telecom companies that have grown rapidly in recent years.

Thirty years ago a mobile telephone probably meant one you could pick up whilst talking and move around the room, even though it still had to be connected to a socket. Today the leading company involved in this industry is worth more than £100 billion! Remarkably, that's over 1,000 times more than it was worth just ten years ago. To invest in these types of companies, you are specifically looking for ones that will replace the current market leaders at the top of the stock market. Rather than paying dividends from profits, these companies normally look to reinvest what profits they make. Some may not even make any profits at all during this growth phase.

Look, for example, at the loss-making Internet access provider Freeserve, and other Internet companies like it. Whatever money it does make will help fund further rapid growth in the business, which will in turn lift its revenues. This, then, will create further value, thus making the stakes of respective shareholders more valuable as well.

Another example of a challenger-style company, which aims to topple the market leaders from their top spots, is Tesco. As mentioned above, this supermarket chain has replaced Sainsburys as the nation's top grocer by market share. This has been achieved by the implementation of a strong strategic plan by superb managers, like Lord MacLaurin. Thirty years ago, Tesco was famed for its pile 'em high, sell 'em cheap policy. MacLaurin instituted the present plan of becoming as renowned for quality as Sainsburys, or indeed Marks and Spencer, whilst maintaining its unique reputation for low prices. Thus in the process Tesco overtook these two rivals.

This shows that such fast-growing companies do not necessarily have to be involved in emerging industries, like mobile telephones. Instead, by implementing fresh ideas, companies operating in established areas can strike out and make up ground on larger and slower rivals. This quick-thinking attribute is probably the one quality common to all leading companies, whether survivors or replacers.

On this basis, now try to predict the leading companies in 2025. We have left a space for you to fill in the prime candidates.

Your list of the top twenty-five companies in 2025

_____

_____

_____

_____

_____

_____

_____

_____

_____

_____

_____

_____

_____

_____

_____

_____

_____

_____

_____

_____

_____

_____

_____

_____

_____

Rule makers and rule breakers

Here at the Motley Fool we divide these two general types of companies into rule makers and rule breakers. Whilst this division works better for the American markets, it can work in the UK as well, as shown above. The survivors make the rules in order to continue their prosperity, and the replacers attempt to usurp the dominant survivors at these coveted top spots by breaking rules.

In brief, rule makers are as near as legally possible to a monopoly. They dominate their market and sector and can effectively control the prices of their product, setting the rules by which rivals run their businesses. Most of them have been around for a while, and look like sticking near the top of the corporate pile for some time to come.

Take good old BT. When the nationalized telecom company was privatized in the mid-1980s and floated on the stock exchange, it held a virtual monopoly over telephone communications in the country. It has faced stiff competition in recent years from start-up mobile operators and other smaller competitors, which have introduced many innovative cabling methods and nifty pricing and connection solutions. But BT has maintained its dominant position.

Indeed, with the development of its mobile arm Cellnet and the rapid growth in data traffic over the Internet, the company has recently managed to swell its profits even further. Remember, this is the group that makes thousands of pounds in profits every second of every day! As consumers we may whinge about BT every now and again. But few of us bother to change our telecom system to a rival. BT still sets the rules in this sector and dominates telecoms in this country, making massive profits. And it looks set to do so for some time.

Looking further afield, the group has built a promising international strategy as well, linking up with giant AT&T of America and with various other companies in Europe and elsewhere. Few young telecom companies make any profit at all at the moment. For example, Orange reported a £98 million loss last year. Meanwhile BT, with billions of pounds in the bank, knocks back all comers that attempt to prod it off its perch.

So in a sense, a decent rule-maker is a company that people hate; yet despite this irrational ire, they continue to use the group's products or services. Such groups are rare corporate beasts indeed. Coca-Cola is a classic example in the US, having consistently lorded it over rival Pepsi for more than fifty years.

The Motley Fool UK has actually chosen BT for its rule shaker real money portfolio. To follow its fortunes and for more information please look at the relevant section of the Web site (**www.fool.co.uk/ruleshaker/ruleshaker.htm**).

That's rule makers covered; so what, you might be wondering, is a rule breaker? To try to find out it's time to take a golf lesson.

Take a golf lesson

Golf is a game with many rules. Professional players break them at their peril. However, successful manufacturers of golf clubs and balls break the regulations governing their industry all the time. Innovators have transformed the game several times using new ideas and technology to the profit of players and investors in such enterprises. In this sense the development of golf equipment illustrates the importance of backing 'rule breakers' when investing.

Rule breakers are emerging companies that come along and shake up the perceived way of doing things in a particular sector or industry. Recent American examples include Internet specialists America Online or Amazon.com. The youthful Wal-Mart, which recently bought UK supermarket chain Asda for £6.7 billion, also broke the ground rules of the retail sector when Sam Walton first came on the scene in the early 1960s.

On the Fool's US site, Foolish founder David Gardner runs a rule breaker portfolio online, dedicated to finding companies conforming to these Foolish credentials. His brother Tom runs a rule maker portfolio. The Gardner brothers have also recently published a book on the subject, called Rule Breakers, Rule Makers.

But now let me take you away from the heady modern-day world of Internet investing and back to St Andrews, the home of golf, in the mid

1840s. At the time, golf was a very minor sport – in fact, sport itself meant racing, hunting, shooting and fishing and little else. The Football Association was not formed until 1863, and the first cricket Test between England and Australia was not scheduled until 1877.

One of the main reasons for this was the lack of leisure time available to most people. A six-day week followed by a Sabbath that was governed by strict religious rules left little time for amusement, except for those that didn't have to work. But golf, apart from being immensely time-consuming, was also expensive. At the time, golf balls, at roughly four shillings each, cost as much as the club used to hit them. Today golf balls cost £2 on average and the most expensive clubs can cost £300.

So losing a ball was disastrous financially. Why were they so expensive? The ones used in the 1840s were called featheries and were handmade. The design had changed little over 300 years. A ball-maker could only make between four and six each day. He took three strips of leather and stitched them together, leaving a small gap through which he stuffed a hatful of wet goose feathers. Hence the name featherie.

Not surprisingly, ball-makers suffered from chronic chest complaints and had short life expectancies. However, as craftsmen they did get to stamp their names on their own balls, and sold them for a healthy price, depending on how well they were made. One of the leading St Andrews makers, Allan Robertson, also the finest player of his generation, sold 2,456 balls in 1844 alone.

However, just four years later Robertson's business caved in dramatically. A St Andrews clergyman, Robert Adam Paterson, was sent an Indian statue of a Hindu god made from gutta-percha. Being a good Christian and a keen golfer, he took a chunk of the latex-like material from the statue and discovered that it could be moulded into a ball shape if softened in hot water. The prototype guttie ball flew much further than a featherie one. The enterprising Paterson immediately took out a patent and sold the manufacturing rights to a London firm.

Golf balls could now be mass-produced by machine for the first time. Thus early gutties sold at a quarter of the price of the featheries and still easily outperformed their handmade predecessors. A fatal blow had been struck to the golf ball industry, revolutionizing it. (Does this ring any bells with the comparison of actively managed funds, handmade by professionals, and passive mechanical index trackers?)

Top featherie-maker Allan Robertson knew the game was up, realizing his product cost four times as much. But in a last ditch effort to preserve his business, he allegedly started to pay caddies at St Andrews sixpence a time to find 'lost' gutties and bring them to him for 'disposal', which meant burning them at night in his workshop.

As a result of Paterson's discovery, golf became much cheaper. An increasingly beneficent legislation, which relaxed working hours and encouraged holidays, and a buoyant economy meant that leisure time concurrently increased. Thus golf, like other sports, boomed in the late nineteenth century, following the boost given by the new rule-breaking guttie ball.

Soon after gutties came in, steel-headed clubs, called 'irons', started to replace the 'long-nosed' wooden-headed implements used previously. Guttie manufacturers and new club makers did very well from this new industry. By the end of the century a staggering £2.6 million was spent on golf each year.

However, gutties themselves came under threat in 1898 when another innovator, American Coburn Haskell, took out a patent for his process of making a rubber-cored golf ball wrapped in a gutta-percha shell. This was the forerunner of the modern three-piece ball. By 1902 it had broken all existing rules to become the dominant ball, with gutties now finding themselves in turn on the scrap heap.

In recent times, two-piece hard-core balls have been introduced and golf club manufacturers have introduced metal-headed (steel and titanium) 'woods'. This has improved many people's games. Callaway, once an innovative club-maker, has been the subject of a recent discussion on the US Fool Web site. Its shares have slipped back so perhaps it is not a dominant rule breaker. Golf has, however, had more than its fair share of this type of company, with the success of Paterson's guttie and Coburn Haskell's modern ball.

You could translate this entrepreneurial tale into virtually any industry. Look, for example, at how the Internet has transformed the book-selling trade both in the US and in this country. Amazon.com started out five years ago from a couple of rooms in Seattle. This revolutionary company can put all books currently in print in an easy electronic catalogue, searchable on Amazon's Web site.

High street book shops cannot compete with this browsing ability. Similarly, book prices have been torn to shreds. Delivery can be much cheaper if there are no branches for Amazon to maintain. Book shop chain WH Smith, for example, is fast losing profits and seeing its business eroded by such online rivals. Last Christmas Amazon registered sales of over $600 million, so you won't be surprised to hear that it has been selected for the US Motley Fool's Rule breaker real money portfolio. Have a look at articles relating to Amazon in this section of the US Fool Web site: **www.fool.com/portfolios/ rulebreaker/rulebreaker.htm**. Other retailers look as if they will come under pressure from online retailers in the future.

Rule breakers exist to take over from current rule makers and displace faltering ones in this category. Many try to do this, but remember, only a few really succeed.

Select your sectors

These investing concepts are all very well, you might think, but you are probably still wondering how exactly to choose which companies to back. Having sorted out your long-term perspective and decided upon the qualities your companies should exhibit, acknowledging that it is impossible to know when exactly to buy, you should now start to whittle down your investment options bearing these three principles in mind.

Let's repeat them:

Sort out your long-term perspective;
Decide upon the qualities your selected companies should exhibit; and
Acknowledge it is impossible to know when exactly to buy.

So, stare ahead twenty-five years and try to think what companies will still be around then. Will people still use banks? What's in store for oil producers? Do you think we will still buy the same old household products and food, via the same methods as today? Will we be connected to the Internet throughout the day? What does this mean for telecom providers?

Of course, nobody really knows exactly how things will pan out, and there's no point in trying to divine the future. However, a good way of trying to find long-stayers is by deciding which sectors might thrive in the early twenty-first century. Then by choosing a correct mix of industries, your choices are made slightly easier.

At the moment the largest industry sectors in London are, in order:

SECTOR	SIZE (BY % OF TOTAL MARKET WEIGHTING)
Telecommunications	14.2%
Banks	12.5%
Oil & Gas	10.1%
Pharmaceuticals	9.6%
Media	6.1%
Life Assurance	3.2%
Software & Computer Services	3.1%
General Retailers	2.9%
Investment Companies	2.9%
Mining	2.5%
Information Technology	2.2%
Transport	2.2%
Support Services	2.1%
Insurance	1.9%
Electrical	1.9%
Food Producers	1.9%
Engineering	1.9%
Construction & Building	1.9%
Leisure, Entertainment & Hotels	1.8%

Beverages	1.7%
Food & Drug Retailers	1.5%
Real Estate	1.4%
Restaurants & Pubs	1.3%
Speciality & Other Finance	1.3%
Gas Distribution	1.2%
Chemicals	1.2%
Aerospace & Defence	1.2%
Water	0.8%
Tobacco	0.7%
Healthcare	0.6%
Electronics	0.6%
Automobiles	0.5%
Distributors	0.4%
Steel & Other Metals	0.3%
Personal Care	0.3%
Forestry & Paper	0.1%
Packaging	0.1%
Household Goods	0.1%
Diversified	0.0%

Which ones will prosper over the next twenty-five years? These general trends should be pretty easy to work out. There will always be producers of staple goods and vital services. For example food manufacturers, utility providers, and transport operators are all going to be necessary. People won't stop eating and requiring heat and electricity or needing to move around.

However, whether such industries can either make more sales than at present, or transact and run their businesses more efficiently, is debatable. What seems to be happening is that only one company from these sectors is thriving at the expense of its rivals. This is the rule maker syndrome in action, where the largest industry player continues to set the pace that others must follow. Consumer prices are falling, cut by the larger companies in an effort to attract even more customers. Smaller players can't afford to do this to the same extent. Thus those with larger volumes of business, and hence greater market share, are succeeding.

However, according to Warren Buffet, in the long run investors value companies according to the profits they make. With prices falling, relative profits in the essential industries will have to drop eventually. This means that only the larger companies with growing sales are succeeding in this field, becoming virtual monopolies in the process.

Sectors where profits look set to grow are in newer areas, where technology is rapidly changing the accepted paradigms. Media companies, telecom companies, software producers and other technically related sectors look set to thrive in this new environment. Of course only a few will ultimately succeed. Cast a brief glance at the most innovative development of the Victorian period: the railway boom. Despite the massive increase in railway building during the nineteenth century, only a handful of companies survived into the twentieth century: a salutary sector lesson indeed.

Place here which sectors you think will be leading, by market value, in 2025:

_____

_____

_____

_____

_____

_____

_____

_____

_____

_____

_____

Having selected the sectors you think will thrive, you must now evaluate the various companies within these fields. This is easier to do now that you can research individual enterprises on the Internet.

E-valuate companies

Notice how, so far, I haven't mentioned share prices once. This is because it is the last thing long-term investors should look at when considering an investment. When you buy a share, you become a part-owner of that enterprise. You may own only one hundred-thousandth of the whole set-up, but nevertheless you can participate in the everyday highs and lows of the business.

So what are you buying, in effect? Well, the technical answer is that you are buying a future stream of the company's earnings. The group may become more profitable than its peers, rewarding you with dividend payments from these profits, or else the company might build its business further, making it more valuable. In the second instance, you feel the company will grow, and hope the money it makes will be reinvested in the business to this end. Then, compared to its peers, it will be more successful, and ownership of it more highly prized than previously.

Also, share prices become almost irrelevant if you intend to hold on to your investment for a considerable period, say at least five or ten years. Blue chip companies' share prices can swing wildly, by as much as 10 per cent on a daily basis. But over the long run, shares in major indices have outperformed all other investments this century. As we discussed when looking at mechanical index trackers in the last chapter, such blue chips have produced an average annual return of 12 per cent.

Some individual companies have inexorably beaten this impressive performance. For instance, since BT floated in 1984, the company has increased in value by an average of 18 per cent each year. That does not include the return you would have got from reinvesting its dividend payments. Therefore to worry when to buy because the share price is moving is ridiculous if you're holding for the long term.

Of course, we'd all like to pick up a bargain. It's incredibly Foolish to get something at a cheaper price than usual, as we showed in Chapter Two on saving cash. But if, in the long run, the value will increase steadily, then short-term fluctuations are irrelevant. This will particularly seem the case when you look back at your initial purchase many years from now. It's like looking across the English Channel and worrying about how the waves offshore from Calais might impact on the white cliffs of Dover days later. Dive in the sea and don't be frightened about such long-distance threats.

If as a connoisseur of art you like a painting now, then buy it, even if people tell you it is overvalued. Trust your instinct that in the future, dealers will be clamouring to get their hands on the work at a significant premium to the price at which you bought it. As with buying a work of art, so we are looking for certain hallmarks in a business, which make it a durable classic within its sector.

In order to find such quality, it is necessary to sift through some fundamental figures using basic analytical tools. So, before making the final plunge, it's time to crunch some numbers and try to discover what stage the business you are looking at has reached. This will help you decide whether it is a fully blossomed rule maker, a budding rule breaker or, of course, neither of these things. In order to do this you need the latest copy of the company's annual report.

You should be able to find this revealing document on the company's Web site, or at least order it there. If not, buy a copy of the *Financial Times* (or go to **FT.com**) and turn to the section at the back that lists all the shares in London. If your company has a playing card club sign, then that means an organization called the Annual Reports club (**www.icbinc.com**) will send you a copy of the latest report. Alternatively, telephone the company secretary, or his office, at the company's headquarters and ask for the report.

When you have received your copy, open it and indulge in the smell of the paper. Careful though, you want to be alert when deciphering the figures inside the report. It's time for the nitty-gritty.

The annual report consists of several sections. The company wants to present its business in the best possible light. Watch out for glossy pictures of the chairman and his board of directors. Don't be distracted by wordy descriptions of the group's products and glowing reviews of the past year. This is all propaganda. Most annual reports show historic records of the company's results over the past five years – particularly if they show an improving trend. Check these out.

The Fool has such data on its Web site, covering the past

three years. The site also has a guide as to how to read an annual report, giving the vital statistics and figures you should be looking for when analysing a company.

The profit and loss statement is perhaps the most informative part of the document. As the name suggests, this will tell you how the company has performed in the past year compared with the same period the year before. Near the top of the columns on this page you will see something called turnover, sometimes referred to as revenue, income or sales. This shows how much in total sales the company made over the last year, or in some cases the level of income or raw revenue it received.

The other important headline figure to bear in mind is profit. This is how much the company had left over from its sales, after stripping out the various costs used to shift the product or provide the service. Because of these various charges and costs, this figure can be represented in many different ways: gross or operating profit; net or pre-tax profit, calculated after taking away financing costs; and profits after tax.

These profits are sometimes called earnings and are worked out on a per share basis (using the post-tax measure). This is most useful when comparing companies in the same sector, of which more later. Normally the most indicative earnings figure is the pre-tax profit calculation, since this gives the most accurate picture of how profitable the company is, after accounting for all types of operating and other charges. Tax charges can vary and do not show how a company is performing.

Now look at the balance sheet, which follows the profit and loss statement. This shows how much, or how little, money the company has to expand its activities. Look for how much cash the company says it has, how much it says it is owed (by companies known as debtors) and also how many debts it owes (called creditors). As with personal loans, debts have to be serviced and these charges can eat into any profits the group makes. The balance sheet also shows the value of the group's goods (stock), fixed assets (property, fittings, equipment and the like) and trademarks or other intellectual properties (intangible assets).

One complaint about balance sheets is that they just give a

snapshot of a company's fiscal health at one particular time of the year. However, the cash flow statement gets around the problem of companies massaging their accounts, by showing how money has moved around over the whole reporting period.

Make things easy – Do them together on message boards and in investment clubs!

You might find this number-crunching process not only tedious but also time-consuming, daunting or even lonely. If this is the case you'll be glad to know that there are ways of combating these symptoms and side effects. Phew!

*There is an individual message board for most large companies on the Motley Fool Web site (**boards.fool.co.uk/Stocks.asp**). There are over 500 company message boards at the moment. Here you will find a variety of people with many different reasons for being interested in a particular company. They may already be shareholders and part-owners of the business. They could, like you, be considering investing in it. They may work in the industry, possibly for the company concerned. Or they may have an interest for other professional or related reasons.*

What matters most is that all these individuals are interested in the company and its business. With so much expertise on offer, learning becomes a fascinating occupation carried out together. This joint endeavour means someone is on hand to offer their opinion and own unique views about how the company is performing. You can take or leave these arguments as you wish. Contribute to the debate or merely watch the proceedings from the touchline. What is sure is that when the company in question releases some interesting information or fresh financial figures, many people will be poring over it and offering their views.

Take the example of one of the most popular boards, the Freeserve board. This group, the largest Internet access provider in the UK, a spin-off from electrical retailer Dixons, has generated an immense amount of debate since it floated in July 1999, setting the benchmark for many other Internet-based companies. Thousands of messages have been contributed to the Freeserve forum, ranging from people working in the industry, shareholders who bought shares in the group at flotation, those who missed out and have a bearish view on the company, and those interested in putting a value on such an innovative enterprise.

Another way of making the investment research process easier and more enjoyable is to join an investment club. You pay a monthly subscription, say £50 per month but perhaps as little as £20, which forms the club's investment fund. Hopefully you encounter a similar range of contributions in your monthly meetings as you would expect to find on a message board. But instead the debates are in the flesh as you decide which investments to back with your club's funds!

The ins and outs of this excellent way of investing have been covered in a Motley Fool book, already published. This is called, unsurprisingly, The Fool's Guide to Investment Clubs. The author, Mark Goodson, also runs a section of the Web site devoted to these incredibly Foolish groups, where you can find out all you need to know about setting up a club.

The experience of joining a club is normally illuminating, educative and fun. It should also be pretty painless. If you subscribe £25 a month, this is less than a pound a day – which is hardly breaking the bank. This is also a way of investing a small amount of money directly in the market, without any of the excessive charges of the Wise. It's a good way to learn about investment before taking the plunge and doing it entirely on your own.

One drawback may be that you can't convince enough friends to form a club with you. You only need five people and can have as many as twenty, so if you can't find a club to join, try posting a message on the Motley Fool's Investment Clubs message board. How Foolish is that?

Having slogged through an annual report, you have now found out how to get basic information about a company and analyse the essential elements of its business. In isolation, this may not be much use. But the true value of the process is that you can now compare the statistics of various companies within your chosen sectors in an effort to decide on the best business to invest in. The following basic analytical techniques will help you roughly choose which stocks stand out from the rest in their field.

Comparisons between companies based on their figures can only be done within sectors. It would be meaningless to try to decide whether top golfer Tiger Woods is a more talented sportsman than tennis star Pete Sampras. What would be the point, apart from fun, of choosing whether the England cricket captain is more proficient than his footballing equivalent? Or indeed saying that Monet's gifts as a painter make his works of art 'better' than Mozart's musical pieces?

Following this principle, it would make little sense to compare the financial attributes of established oil company Shell with growing mobile phone provider Vodafone. Their two industries are like chalk and cheese, requiring companies with different capabilities and different reactions to overriding economic issues. However, it would be perfectly reasonable to compare Shell with its rival BP Amoco, and similarly to make direct comparisons between Vodafone and Orange, both of whom operate in exactly the same field.

In the last chapter, when we talked about the mechanical Beating The Footsie strategy, we mentioned the dividend yield. This was a way of finding the relatively cheaper companies by seeing which ones paid a more generous dividend. A related way of comparing companies' cheapness is by looking at the ratio between their respective earnings and their share price. This is known as the PE ratio for short. The P stands for the price per share (or share price) and the E for earnings per share.

A few pages back, we mentioned the earnings per share figure as one of the ways profits are displayed in an annual report. Now different companies have differing numbers of shares in issue. A company's share price is calculated by dividing its total market value (sometimes called the market capitalization or 'cap' for short) by the number of shares in issue. This is similar to the way the earnings per share are calculated: by dividing the total post-tax earnings (profits) by the number of shares in issue. So, then, by dividing the price per share by the earnings by share, you should arrive at a PE ratio. This can now be used to see how highly prized the market thinks one company is over another. Higher PE ratios suggest that buying this stream of earnings will cost more than buying those of a company with a lesser PE ratio.

Thus at the time of writing in January 2000, BP Amoco's share price is 556p and rival Shell's is 485p. On their own you could not say that one share is 'cheaper' or, to put it another way, better value than the other. (No, Shell is not cheaper just because it has a lower share price ...) However, BP's earnings per share in 1999 were 8.2p and Shell's were 10.8p. Again, these figures mean nothing in isolation, but if you divide BP's price per share (556p) by its earnings per share (8.2p), you arrive at a PE ratio of sixty-eight. Do the same for Shell and you get a PE of forty-five. Therefore, on these rough calculations, shares in BP Amoco are almost 50 per cent more expensive to buy than Shell shares, going on their earnings from last year.

In comparison, Vodafone's PE ratio is far higher at ninety-nine. This is because its business is growing at a far quicker rate than established oil producers like Shell or BP. Orange does not even make a profit yet, so its PE ratio is infinite! Thus this conventional method of valuing companies works better when applied to more established industries and businesses than to fast-growing sectors.

A preferable way of deciding whether one business is better than another within an industry sector is by looking at their profit margins. This can be done even for a group that makes no pre-tax profit, as it is likely to make an operating profit from its sales – unless, of course, it makes no sales, like a biopharmaceutical company researching a drug to cure a particular ailment. By dividing the operating profit (found in the annual report) by the turnover figure, you can compare how profitable, or more efficient, one business is compared with others in its sector.

Take Vodafone. This telecom company made £847 million in operating profits from total sales of £3,360 million in 1999. If you divide the operating profits by the sales, this gives Vodafone an operating margin of 25 per cent. Orange, on the other hand, reported a £16 million operating profit in 1998, despite showing a £98 million pre-tax loss (after accounting for other funding charges) on a total turnover of £1,213 million. This gives it an operating margin of just 1.3 per cent!

Of course in this instance we are not comparing exact accounting years and this skews our results. And with such a fast-paced industry, encountering many dramatic changes, it is next to impossible to do any accurate analysis. In any case this should be done over several years and not just one.

If this detailed analysis interests you, and we hope it does because selecting winning rule makers and rule breakers is at the heart of securing long-term wealth, then the Fool has written in abundance on these topics in tomes that are suitably fun, frivolous and Foolish. *The Motley Fool UK Investment Workbook* is most useful. And the Motley Fool Web site is a veritable cornucopia of Foolish thought as well, receiving thousands of contributions on the message boards daily.

Ultimately, though, share analysis is an inaccurate science. It provides only a rough guide to selecting suitable companies to invest in. So take frequent breaks, and give your more artistic instinct free rein to think creatively about the direction of the world in the future.

Long-term buy and hold: why investing isn't gambling

If you are trying to choose a horse to back in a particular race, your 'investment' in that particular beast will only last ten minutes at most. If the nag fails to win, then you will lose your whole stake. That's why gambling on the races doesn't pay, particularly in the short term and normally in the long term as well.

Now imagine if you were forced to invest for your future, but were not allowed to buy shares and could only back horses. Rather than trying to select a winner from each race, perhaps a more sensible strategy would be to find a successful trainer, or jockey, who usually enjoyed a better success rate than his fellow professionals. Back this selected individual over his whole career and at least your losses would be slightly curtailed. (Bookmakers set the odds so that over the long run they will always be guaranteed a profit from their activities).

Apply this beloved betting principle to the investment arena, and you should be able to see the benefits of following one professional outfit over the long term. Take a large drug company. Let's call it Pill Poppers. This group has a number of different products in its stable. Some perform better than others. These are thus more popular, sell more for the company, recoup their development (and running) costs more easily and make the company more profitable.

Other drugs fail at some stage of their development process, or do not sell as strongly as anticipated, perhaps because equivalent products made by rival companies remain more effective and popular. Overall these products might cost Pill Poppers money. Nevertheless, as long as the management of the company can ensure that the popular pills outperform and offset the losses incurred from the dud drugs, then in the long run the company will outlive the peaks and troughs and prosper profitably.

Thus if you hold shares in the company for some time, your stake should become more valuable as profits continue to be made. And what's more, unlike gambling where you lose your stake if you don't win, unless something goes drastically wrong you should retain your original capital stake as well.

DRiP schemes: cheap and easy ways of investing in shares directly

One way of avoiding the peaks and troughs of performance when investing in shares is to invest a small amount regularly, say each month. This method, known as pound-cost averaging, was explained when we looked at index-tracking funds in the chapter on mechanical investments. Many providers of such index followers will allow individuals to feed as little as £50 per month into the fund to buy as many units as possible at the time of payment.

In America, over a thousand companies also allow individual investors to purchase small amounts of shares via similar methods. Yes, that's right, you can feed in say £25 a month and this will buy a certain number of shares in the company of your choice.

For long-term investors in leading companies with stable records, this eliminates any worries about when to buy, or concerns that a share is 'too expensive'. Instead, by steadily feeding in regular amounts, you can build up a substantial holding at a price that is never too high or too low.

What's more, and this is where such schemes become really Foolish, you can buy these shares directly from the company concerned, without the intervention of any Wise broker at all! Wave goodbye to commission and exorbitant fees. Hoorah!

These tremendous tools are called Dividend Reinvestment Programmes (DRiPs) or Direct Share Plans (DSPs). Throughout this book, we have discussed the wonderful long-term return offered by shares. These returns are calculated after any dividends given out by companies have been reinvested in further shares. Many companies used to offer shareholders 'scrips'. These mini-share issues allowed you to take the dividend payment in new shares rather than cash. This made it easy to reinvest dividends to maximize your long-term returns. But recently, most companies have paid their dividends in cash.

However, the American fashion for DRiPs and DSPs is beginning to take off in this country. As said above, thousands of US companies run them. The Motley Fool in the States actually runs a real money portfolio on its Web site that invests only via these Foolish schemes. In the UK, DRiPs are currently more popular than DSPs. As the name suggests, these allow you to reinvest the dividends in the company, rather than taking the cash payment. In order to enroll you generally have to be on the shareholder register.

Be careful, therefore, not to open a nominee account with a broker! You only need buy one share, through a broker, but remember to ask for it to be on a CREST account or even better to receive a share certificate. CREST is a paperless settlement system, so shares can change hands electronically without the need for share certificates. You will need to send this share certificate, or electronic equivalent, to the company running the DRiP to enroll in the scheme.

The Share Centre (a low-cost dealer you can contact on 01442 890800) will let you invest in one share for a £2.50 charge, and *will give you a certificate for £15. But splashing out on this certificate is not worth it because the Share Centre will agree to reinvest all dividends of FTSE 100 shares automatically, if you specify that you require this service.*

The beauty of many DRiPs is that you can make Optional Cash Payments on many of them. This method will let you drip in regular monthly amounts to buy shares. DSPs operate along these lines as well, but without the need to get on the shareholder register. DSPs are not common in the UK at present.

As mentioned above, not all FTSE 100 companies offer DRiPs yet. Obviously, only those that pay dividends will organize them. Looking at the top twenty-five companies, almost half (BP Amoco, BT, HSBC, Shell, Astra Zeneca, SmithKline Beecham, Barclays, NatWest, Diageo, Rio Tinto, and Unilever) offer DRiP schemes for their American investors. Most of these have also opened up their schemes to domestic UK investors. Some still charge quite a bit to buy additional shares. So in some cases buying shares directly is not the most economic move, although you will still get the benefit of pound-cost averaging.

Here at the Fool, we hope all the leading dividend-paying companies within the FTSE 100 will soon offer DRiPs to encourage long-term investment. To find out whether a company you are interested in does so, ring the group's registrar, who deals with shareholder queries, or else ring the relevant company secretary direct. This is another Foolish campaign to fight. And you won't be surprised to discover that there is a Motley Fool UK message board devoted to the subject of DRiPs.

Before rounding off this brief introduction to the Foolish realm and letting you loose on **www.fool.co.uk** to meet other Fools in the playground, there are a few other areas you might like to consider.

As the world becomes ever smaller, within a few years it will be possible to invest in any company around the globe. As a Fool on the Web site has said, you should 'treat the world as your investment arena'. Already, it is quite easy to buy shares in American companies directly. The range on offer will only increase, opening up tremendous opportunities for individual investors.

Also, remember that there are numerous mistakes to make when investing. Never be too confident and always go back to Foolish basics if you come unstuck. With a solid Foolish financial footing you can't go too far wrong. Treat mistakes as an opportunity to learn. Profit from them in some way, however hard this may seem at the time.

And above all have fun. Life is too short to be Wise!

Ten Foolish steps towards starting to invest directly in shares:

1. The investment arena has rarely looked as promising and inviting for individual investors in companies.
2. Thanks to the Internet, private investors have access to as much information as professionals.
3. The charges incurred from dealing in shares has progressively fallen. Discount brokers offer deals charging on average 1 per cent commission.
4. Investment principles remain the same as ever. Take a look at the methods of successful investors such as Warren Buffet.
5. Research the future: compare the top companies of twenty-five years ago with those of today. From this try and think what companies will be thriving twenty-five years from now.
6. Rulemakers consistently remain at the top of the pile and are inventive enough to hold their position easily against all-comers.
7. Rulebreakers challenge for these coveted top spots by breaking rules to usurp these dominant survivors.
8. Select your sectors: choose what industries will prosper over the coming years.
9. E-valuate companies: analyse these companies using the Internet and annual reports.
10. Make things easy: work together on message boards and investment clubs.

Conclusion: Then you'll be a Fool my son…

Who's the more foolish, the fool, or the fool who follows him?
Obi-Wan Kenobi, *Star Wars*

Thank you for following me on this Foolish trip. If you have any queries or comments, please send them on to: **Nomoney@fool.co.uk**. Alternatively, post a message on the board dedicated to discussing this book.

Now, hopefully, having organized your finances, you feel in a more confident position to go out and invest directly. But remember this is only the beginning of your journey. With a Foolish foundation, you should be able to confront all that lies ahead of you. With that in mind, here's a final Foolish offering to send you on your way …

Several years ago, the BBC ran a poll to find the nation's favourite poem. Kipling's 'If' topped the list. It was easy to see why. Kipling wrote 'If' as an educational poem from a father to his son about how to 'succeed' in life. Not surprisingly, many schools latched on to Kipling's coat-tails and 'If' was quickly established as a popular poem to recite in classes up and down the land throughout the last century.

Fools would do well to go back and take a look at the poem again. It gives many Foolish lessons about how to survive financially in a Wise and wicked world. But to save you the trouble, here is a Foolishly adapted version of 'If', which may help to outline Foolish ways for proto-Fools.

'If
(with apologies to Rudyard Kipling)

If you can keep your head when all about you
Are losing theirs and blaming recent news;
If you can trust yourself when many doubt your views,
But make allowance for their doubting too;
If you can wait and not be tired by waiting,
Or, being lied to, don't deal in lies,
Or, seeing 'sells', don't give way to selling,
And yet don't act too bold, nor talk too Wise;

If you can dream – and not make dreams your master;
If you can think – and make research your aim;
If you can meet with triumph and disaster
And treat those two imposters just the same;
If you can bear to hear the truth you've spoken
Twisted by the Wise to make a trap for Fools,
Or watch unit trusts you gave your cash to broken,
And use instead your own investment tools;

If you can make one heap of surplus earnings
And risk it on the market's pitch-and-toss,
And lose, and start again near your beginnings
And learn a Foolish lesson from your loss;
If you can force your heart and nerve and wallet
To hold your shares long after they have doubled,
And so hold on when there is nothing in you
Except the Will which says to them: 'Hold on!';

If you can talk with crowds and keep your virtue,
Or e-mail chairmen – nor lose the common touch;
If neither broker buys nor sells can hurt you;
If all views count with you, but none too much;
If you can fill the unforgiving minute
With sixty seconds' worth of message fun –
Yours is the Earth and everything that's in it,
And – which is more – you'll be a Fool my son!

Acknowledgements

The motto of the Motley Fool is to 'educate, amuse and enrich'. I'd like to thank all those who've educated me at school and university, especially historians; the many friends who have amused me throughout my life so far, particularly Lucy; and my father for enriching my life no end. Daddy, you have always been the biggest Fool I know! In addition I'd also like to thank David Berger, Bruce Jackson and all at Fool UK for their ongoing Folly and for making it all possible.

No man is so foolish, but may give another good counsel some-
times; and no man is so wise, but may easily err, if he will take
no others' counsel, but his own. But very few men are wise by
their own counsel; or learned by their own teaching. For he that
was only taught by himself, had a fool to his Master.
Ben Jonson, 'Timber'